Moving at the Speed of Grace

Moving at the Speed of Grace is a powerful book and has made a profound impact on me both as a person and as a basketball coach. Ramsey's use of modern day parables inspires me, and I plan to incorporate several of his principles into our team handbook. Read it, and you too will be moved!

—Beth Dunkenberger,
head coach of the Virginia Tech women's basketball team

Another appropriate title for Norman Ramsey's *Moving at the Speed of Grace* could be "moving at the speed of Scripture." This book is filled with Holy Scripture and biblical content. It is also filled with wonderful personal stories that illustrate the steps along the way of grace. Preachers will find the book worth the price because of the stories and the many insightful questions. I have long believed that stories inform and questions transform—engaging adult readers and learners in the essential process of theological reflection. The book helped me to grow and to move forward in my own spiritual journey...

—Tom Albin,
dean of The Upper Room Chapel, Nashville, TN

Norman Ramsey has done an excellent job in writing about a subject that is common to all humanity. It is written in very understandable language, clear, filled with good illustrations and with sharing his life and family. *Moving at the Speed of Grace* will make learning in small groups very exciting. The suggested study questions are relevant to life present and future.

—Dr. Evelyn Laycock,
former director of the Lay Ministry Center in Lake Junaluska, NC

Moving at the Speed of Grace

Ray:

The grace & joy of Jesus

be your un avordable experience!

Norman Ramsey

2 Tim 2.

NORMAN RAMSEY

Moving at the Speed of Grace

DISCOVERING THE
WAY GOD WORKS

TATE PUBLISHING & Enterprises

All scripture quotations, unless otherwise indicated, are taken from the *Holy Bible, New International Version®* NIV®. Copyright 1973, 1978, 1984 by International Bible Society. Used by permission of Zondervan. All rights reserved.

Scripture quotations marked (KJV) are taken from the *Holy Bible, King James Version*, Cambridge, 1769. Used by permission. All rights reserved.

Scripture quotations marked NKJV are taken from the *New King James Version®*. Copyright © 1982 by Thomas Nelson, Inc. Used by permission. All rights reserved.

The Message by Eugene H. Peterson, copyright © 1993, 1994, 1995, 1996, 2000, 2001, 2002. Used by permission of NavPress Publishing Group. All rights reserved.

Within scripture verses, notes added by the author are enclosed in [brackets].

The opinions expressed by the author are not necessarily those of Tate Publishing, LLC.

Published by Tate Publishing & Enterprises, LLC
127 E. Trade Center Terrace | Mustang, Oklahoma 73064 USA
1.888.361.9473 | www.tatepublishing.com

Tate Publishing is committed to excellence in the publishing industry. The company reflects the philosophy established by the founders, based on Psalm 68:11,
"The Lord gave the word and great was the company of those who published it."

Book design copyright © 2010 by Tate Publishing, LLC. All rights reserved.
Cover design by Kandi Evans
Interior design by Stephanie Woloszyn

Published in the United States of America
ISBN: 978-1-61663-501-5
1. Religion / Christian Theology / General   2. Religion / Christianity / General
10.05.06

ACKNOWLEDGMENTS

No project like this is a solitary endeavor. It is a re-gift, not because it has been unused but because it has been used so much. The Bible says freely we have received so freely we give, and I must acknowledge the gift of grace the Lord has given me in writing this book. Most of all I give thanks for the way it has helped me remember and appreciate the life of my father. My daddy, Norman L. Ramsey, Jr., died of stomach cancer just as God's pathway of grace was taking root in my heart and mind. In our last conversation, he encouraged my dream of sharing God's way of working with you.

This book is dedicated to his memory and to God's way of working in him and in my mother. Without the wisdom and generosity of family and friends, I never would have been awake or alert to what I share in this book.

My family is special. Janet and J.B., Dennis and Lisa, and Teresa have all driven me forward in their own way. My beautiful wife, Karen, is God's best gift to me. She and all my children: Sandra, Keith, Robert, and Hannah have graciously waited for Daddy's book to come out.

God also sent special friends into my life just when I needed them the most. Rick Bonfim confirmed my wild thoughts about God's grace and was an instrument of God's healing in my life. He and Betty McKinney and our ministry trips to Brazil have forever changed my life. When I wanted to actually begin writing something, God introduced me to Glenn Dietzel and Ronda Del Boccio. Ronda's encouragement to me has kept me going many times.

I thank the Lord for all the church members in the places where I have served—in North Carolina, Kentucky, Tennessee, and Virginia. I especially have to thank the people of White Memorial UMC and South Hill UMC. You heard me and loved me and allowed me to preach this onto paper. You have become part of who I am. I have to thank Mitch Sutphin. Without our breakfasts together, I never would have understood the parable of the pancake. Miss K. K. and I love you and your family very much.

I want you to know how much Gerald Bowles means to me. Gerald is a great friend, a member of the ministry's board of directors, and an insightful and humble man of God. Gerald's reading and critiquing of *Moving at the Speed of Grace* has made this a better book and made me a better Christian. He and the other member's of our ministry board, Larry Craddock and Bob Woolke, have been very supportive of me. Thanks, too, to Karen Williams for the first edit of the book and for the Rev. Tim Irving who read the book multiple times and formulated the questions at the end of each chapter. Also, special thanks go to John Eldredge, Ken Fisher, Dave Ramsey, and Mark Tier who gave me permission to interpret their ministries into mine. Thanks, as well to Dr. Richard Tate and Tate Publishing for wanting to share my words as well as my music.

Table of Contents

Our Preamble up the Pathway of Grace

Enter through the narrow gate. For wide is the gate and broad is the road that leads to destruction, and many enter through it. But small is the gate and narrow the road that leads to life, and only a few find it.

Matthew 7:13–14

The wages of sin is death, but the gift of God is eternal life in Christ Jesus our Lord.

Romans 6:23

Two roads diverged in a wood, and I—
I took the one less traveled by,
And that has made all the difference.

—Robert Frost, "The Road Not Taken"

HOW IT ALL BEGAN

And we know that in all things God works for the good of those who love him, who have been called according to his purpose. For those God foreknew he also predestined to be conformed to the likeness of his Son, that he might be the firstborn among many brothers. And those he predestined, he also called; those he called, he also justified; those he justified, he also glorified.

Romans 8:28–30

The story of this book began as a sermon I preached on the first Sunday in January 2004. I was serving White Memorial United Methodist Church, and we were beginning the year with the goal of reading and preaching through the scriptures. I preached on "The Pathway of Grace: The Way God Always Follows," using Romans 8:28–30 and Genesis 1 as the scriptural texts. I used Genesis to describe the pathway sin always takes. (The outline of that path is in Appendix A.)

Jesus was familiar with the pathway of grace and the pathway of sin and compared them in Matthew 7:13–14: "Enter through the narrow gate. For wide is the gate that leads to destruction and many enter through it. But small is the gate and narrow the road that leads to life and only a few find it." This book is written to help you to be among those who find and follow the way of life.

I am convinced that "Jesus is the same yesterday, today, and forever" and has a method of operation (Hebrews 13:8). This conviction has come to me gradually but with increasing intensity and clarity. As we progressed through the Bible in 2004, I began to notice the turns in the path of sin and the path of grace which were emerging in the characters and situations in the scripture. I began to see the path of grace represented in Romans 8:28–30 and reinforced in Romans 8:31–37. I saw the pathway of grace emerge in Psalm 23, the Lord's Prayer, and in Ephesians 6 as we are called to put on the whole armor of God. I noticed the contours of that grace path in Isaiah 12. The path of grace was outlined when God gave direction for blessing in Numbers 6.

Yet, the more I observed, the more doubts I had. I thought I must be making this up—seeing things because I want to see them. For over a year and a half these paths of sin and grace appeared to be demonstrated to me through the scripture and in everyday conversations. I needed confirmation. Surely if this is the way God moves, it is being revealed to more than just me. Thankfully, it had been.

In July 2005, I attended an Aldersgate Renewal Ministry event. At a seminar on ministering to people effectively at the altar, I listened as Rick Bonfim explained the four places where people get stuck in sin. These four places were the first four downturns of the path God had shown me. He used a few different words than I had, but the substance was the same.

RICK'S	MINE
rejection	betrayal
rebellion	bias
unforgiveness	blame
bitterness	bitterness

I decided I needed to spend some time with Rick, so I committed to going on a Brazil mission trip with him. It's one of the best decisions I ever made. Under the anointed teaching and praying of Rick Bonfim and Betty McKinney, I found freedom from a lifetime of lies I had believed about myself. It was there in Brazil that the path, especially as it is given in Romans 8:28–30, became substantial enough in me to begin to communicate with others.

God brought me gradually over those first two years to under-stand the pathway of his grace. I offer this book to speed you in walking the pathway of grace. God understands you and knows you. The Bible says he broke down the wall between us through Jesus Christ. Do you desire to close the gap between your actions and God's? If so, my hope is that this study will help. The scripture says: "As you learn more and more how God works, you will learn how to do your work" (Colossians 1:10, *The Message*). This path will not give you fast and easy steps to unavoidable, spiritual success. There are no such steps.

Jesus said:

> Don't look for shortcuts to God. The market is flooded with sure-fire, easygoing formulas for a successful life that can be practiced in your spare time. Don't fall for that stuff, even though crowds of people do. The way to life—to God!—is vigorous and requires total attention.
>
> Matthew 7:13–14 (The Message)

What I am trusting will happen as you read this book will be a growing awareness in your spirit, soul, and body of how God works. I'm also trusting that as God reveals his ways to you, it will whet your appetite to "hunger and thirst after righteousness" even more (Matthew 5:6).

What this path will show you is that Jesus calls us on purpose. Everything Jesus does has an objective. The Bible teaches Jesus is the "author and finisher of our faith"—the Trailblazer who calls us to follow (Hebrews 12: 2, KJV). The aim of this book is to show that Jesus cuts the trail of redemption a certain way. The trail is blazed to save us from being lost, to draw us away from the dead end to which sin takes us, and to direct us towards fullness of life in the Spirit. The path towards this fullness Jesus wants you to experience is outlined by the Apostle Paul in Romans 8:28–30:

And we know that in all things God works for the good of those who love him, who have been called according to his purpose. For those God foreknew he also predestined to be conformed to the likeness of his Son, that he might be the firstborn among many brothers. And those he predestined, he also called; those he called, he also justified; those he justified, he also glorified.

See, the source of our faith and the ground of our hope is this: God is at work. Hear that. Let that register in your soul. God is at work. This truth, this undeniable fact of faith, is what gives us the power and the confidence to step onto the pathway of grace. This purpose statement of God's righteousness ("In all things God works for the good of those who love him") is the springboard upon which we leap out to follow the pathway of grace.

THE PATHWAY OF GRACE

Following the pathway of grace is how you live out God's purpose for your life. Romans 8:28b–30 spells out the path upon which God will carry you. Before anything, God loves us and gave his only, begotten Son for us. We become aware of that great love when we hear God's call. "And we know that in all things God works for the good of those who love him, *who have been called according to his purpose*" (Romans 8:28).

God gives an invitation. "Turn around; you're going the wrong way." "May I have your attention, please?" This is a generic call to everyone, to "whosoever" will. Jesus radically offers this call every time he says, "Follow me." The prophet Isaiah said, "Whether you turn to the right or the left, your ears will hear a voice behind you saying, 'This is the way; walk in it'" (Isaiah 30:21). Or as my friend shared, "Here is the path, dummy!"

Those God calls he also foreknew. This word implies that left to ourselves we would not find the path or be able to walk it to its promised end. But, God would work, and we could respond. God believed in us before we ever believed in God. We could live by faith. God said "yes" to you. You can now say "yes" to God.

Those whom God foreknew, he also predestined to be conformed into the likeness of his Son. Life is not a journey of self-improvement. It is a journey of self-denial where we become strong through surrender, mighty through meekness, faithful through forgiveness, finding everything we need by casting all our cares on Jesus.

Those God predestined, he also called. This call is different from the first. It is more a special assignment than a general invitation. It is God's whisper to you: "I have a job only you can do." This is the conversation of two friends as they move along together.

Those God called, he also justified. Have you ever hesitated when a special opportunity arose? Offered excuses rather than excitement? This word is for you. It simply means you are free to go, free to fulfill what God has whispered. As you respond, "I can do all things through Christ who strengthens me," God has more.

Those God justifies, he also glorifies. Because Jesus was raised from the dead, you can rise to any occasion. You can walk the pathway of grace. You can mature. You can breakthrough the barriers that life presents and move forward in repentance, believing what God says about you and building up your most holy faith. You can become a blessing to others, taking responsibility for the entirety of your life. You can become a person of influence, a person whose strength is renewed day by day.

I state this outline to help you remember it. It was the outline I followed in that first sermon January 2004. We will revisit it over and over again. It is:

1. Begin in repentance

2. Believe in the Lord Jesus

3. Build up your most holy faith

4. Bless

5. Bring life

6. Breakthrough

This is the path God follows. It is the pathway of God's grace. These six Bs are the markers for our journey. Following them, we will each become the person we were meant to be! These six Bs mark our course and chart our way. Let them give you practical help in understanding how God wants to accomplish his eternal purposes in you. This is not something new. It's something you have done before. You don't remember?

CAN YOU TIE MY SHOES FOR ME?

Can you tie my shoes for me? Before I could ever ask the question, my mom and dad tied my shoes for me. But there was a different kind of joy and delight when, as a small child, I asked the question for the first time, "Can you help me tie my shoes?" From this point we moved forward together. The shoes still needed lacing up, but now we bent over together; my parents were the trusted authority. They placed hands in the right spot. They spoke the words, "Good job! Way to go!" They provided the encouragement, "You are getting better and better. You can do it."

Their encouragement was twofold. It moved me toward a sense of accomplishment and toward a greater sense of awareness. The accomplishment is "I've learned to tie my shoes." The sense of awareness was to notice when others needed help, instruction, or encouragement in tying their shoes. My parents' joy was transferred when I came back from first grade one day and told them how I had tied Matthew Petty's shoes for him. I noticed he didn't know how to tie them up, and I told him I could help him. I said, "My mama and daddy taught me how to do it. I'll teach you."

This simple story about tying shoes illustrates the pathway of grace. It began in repentance as I asked for help; showed itself in trust as I stuck out my foot depending on Mama and Daddy. I built up my faith, watching and waiting, bent over together with my parents until I could do it for myself. I moved into blessing as I noticed Matthew Petty. I brought life and light as he learned and enjoyed that same sense of accomplishment I had felt. The breakthrough occurred when I saw Matthew, the new tier-of-shoes, teach someone else. A life had been transformed and mine had too.

Become familiar with this pattern, the pathway of grace. Listen for it. Look for it. Get a handle on it. Why? The answer is because there is a path with which you are already familiar—the pathway of sin.

THE PATHWAY OF SIN

We have all been on the pathway of sin. The prophet Isaiah said, "We all, like sheep, have gone astray, each of us has turned to his own way; and the Lord has laid on him (Jesus) the iniquity of us all" (Isaiah 53:6). We don't want the sacrifice of Jesus to be in vain. We are to walk a new path, opened up for us by and through Jesus. But to walk that new path, I'll lay out the path sin follows, as well.

1. Betrayal

2. Bias

3. Blame

4. Bitterness

5. Bloodshed

6. Breaking point

Recognize it for what it is: a place to get off as quickly as possible. As you become more familiar with the pathway of grace, the pathway of sin will become much more clearly defined. This is good news. You can avoid stumbling when you see exactly what is trying to trip you or make you fall. Thus, you will become more sure-footed spiritually, your blind spots will become smaller, and your ability to hear God's word will be heightened. You won't waste as much time moving towards repentance. You'll simply choose to turn away and step off the pathway of sin. You will become a faithful follower of the pathway of grace. This is my prayer for you.

WHICH WAY ARE YOU GOING?

We are all creatures of habit. How many of you on your way home from work were supposed to stop off somewhere, but it was only when you pulled into the driveway you remembered you forgot? A couple of months before Karen and I were married, we were driving toward home one day. We were supposed to make a left turn about five miles from home to go get my haircut. But we were talking and very much in love. When I flipped on my right turn signal to go down our street, I realized I had gone four miles too far. We turned around, started talking again, and only missed the turn by a quarter of a mile. We turned around again, started talking, and managed to stop just in time to back up and make our left turn.

I share this to let you know that no matter how many times you miss the mark, you can get turned around in the right direction. This book is written for your comfort. Reading it, you will learn how God works. You will become so familiar with it that to turn off of it will be completely out of place. You will deepen your relationship of trust in Jesus. You'll fall so in love with him that many things that used to distract and damage your relationship with Jesus and others, won't affect you anymore. You will drive right by them. You will not be turned aside. You will know how to act with more confidence. The fragrance of love, joy, and peace will be the lingering impression you will leave in every place you go. Freedom will mark your every step. The security of your standing with Jesus will not be shaken.

So get ready to give Jesus your total attention. Get ready to move at the speed of grace!

SMALL GROUP DISCUSSION QUESTIONS

1. As you begin reading this book, take some time to look at your spiritual life. What have been the highlights, and where have you struggled the most?

2. Think about the people you know who have grown in their spiritual life. What do you admire about them?

3. From what you have read so far, what do you feel God is saying to you?

4. Are you willing to invest in learning about the pathway of grace in order to grow in your spiritual life?

Share your answers with your group.

Follow Jesus

But Jesus told him, "Follow me."

Matthew 8: 22

Jesus answered, "I am the Way and the Truth and the Life. No one comes [or makes progress] to the Father except through me."

John 14:6

Let us fix our eyes on Jesus, the author and perfecter of our faith, who for the joy set before him endured the cross, scorning its shame, and sat down at the right hand of the throne of God.

Consider him who endured such opposition from sinful men, so that you will not grow weary and lose heart.

Hebrews 12:2–3

JESUS: OUR POINT OF ORIGIN

Go to Mapquest® to get directions for a trip. You will need two things: a starting and an ending location. This is who Jesus is for us. How can we expect to walk the path until we see it modeled for us? This is why we consider Jesus before starting down the path ourselves. Jesus alone perfectly embodies and follows the pathway of grace. Without Jesus Christ, anyone trying to walk the pathway of grace will only fall short in the journey. Jesus must become our trusted guide, and we must become his trusting companion.

One of the first persons to point out why we need Jesus was Zechariah, the father of John the Baptist. He had an encounter with an angel as he served in the temple. Skeptical of the angel's promise, he was put on mute until the promise came true. Finally, that day came. Zechariah was asked to write and confirm the name *John* for his newborn son. When he did, his voice returned. Zechariah was filled with the Holy Spirit, and he prophesied (Luke 1:67). His prophecy concerned the coming Messiah. His prophecy was all about Jesus. His prophecy also follows the pathway of grace. Because this is such an important message, it is magnified by being repeated (Read Luke 1:68–79.). God often repeats his ways to emphasize them. Sometimes it takes a lot of repetition to see things God's way. As Jesus said, we are sometimes "slow of heart to believe" (Luke 24: 25).

1. We *begin* in repentance and worship. We praise the Lord God of Israel for coming to us (v. 68). In Jesus' coming, he is the incarnate Way of the Most High (v. 76). As the hymn *Joy to the World* says, "Let every heart prepare him room."

2. We *believe* in the Savior whom God has sent (v. 69). "This

is the work of God: that you believe on him whom God has sent" (John 6:29). Zechariah prophesies that his son John the Baptist will make God's people know that they can be saved (v. 77).

3. We *build* up our faith by remembering God's promise (v. 70) to save us from our enemies, from the power of all who hate us (v. 71), and untangle us from our sin (v. 77)

4. We *bless* others because God has blessed us and shown us his mercy (vv. 72–73). Jesus comes as the tender mercy of God incarnate (v. 78).

5. We *bring* life to others because God has not only drawn us out of the hand of our enemy, but also has poured out his Holy Spirit to bring us newness of life (v. 74). In Jesus Christ, God has come to baptize us with the Holy Spirit and fire. The Dayspring from on High has come. He shines on us and we share his light with those who still sit in darkness (vv. 78–79).

7. We *breakthrough* into a life that is made new each day. We serve the Lord without fear in holiness and righteousness (v. 75). Jesus is Lord and leads us in the way of peace (v. 79).

These six stages form the outline of the book. This is the pathway of grace. Zechariah is prophesying how Jesus will come. Jesus will come following the pathway of grace.

Think about these verses, and let's put them together with Romans 8:28–30. Stay with me here. Be alert. Notice the progression. We are rehearsing the way God works.

1. God comes to us and calls us in repentance to walk in the way Jesus is opening for us.

2. God foreknows what is necessary for us to experience fullness of life, so God reveals and raises Jesus for our salvation.

3. Salvation applied to our lives untangles us from our sin and brings us into conformity with Christ.

4. God shows us mercy, remembers and blesses us, so we can hear his call and do the same for others.

5. God frees us from our limitations, shines on us, justifying us as good to go.

6. Finally, God glorifies us, enables us to serve him, and teaches us the path of peace

As we follow the pathway of grace, we now move forward in repentance. We see new ways God is coming to us and opening in us. Our faith and trust are deeper, more multifaceted. We're growing in our understanding. Our devotion finds new avenues of expression. We are led by the Spirit to bless others, more quickly sensing and responding to the core need. We are much quicker to humble ourselves and allow the work of God in others to flourish. We see that Paul was right: "godliness with contentment is great gain" (1 Timothy 6:6).

We will begin to notice our vocabulary and our reactions to things in light of this path. We will remember each turn along the way. As Romans 8:31–39 reminds us, we will remember God is for us. We will remember the One, who did not spare his own Son, will graciously give us all things. We will remember it is God who answers every charge against us. We don't have to justify ourselves anymore. We remember God is at work accomplishing his will through us for the sake of others. Nothing can separate us from his love, so we are more than conquerors through Jesus Christ.

Jesus Is the Way-Maker

What does it mean that Jesus is the Way and the Way-Maker? First, it means that God is taking the initiative in providing a solution for breaking us free from being rooted in sin. Jesus said, "Just as Moses lifted up the serpent in the wilderness so the Son of Man must also be lifted up that everyone who believes in him may have eternal life" (John 3:14–15). Look at Numbers 21. The people were under the curse of death because of their iniquity. God told Moses to create a brazen serpent, and if anyone would focus on it, healing and deliverance would come.

When John sees Jesus, John tells his disciples, "Behold the Lamb of God who takes away the sin of the world" (John 1:29, KJV). Read Genesis 22. Abraham is commanded by God to sacrifice the son whom he loves. In the midst of that trial, Abraham, hoping against hope, says, "God will provide himself a lamb for the sacrifice" (Genesis 22:8). Portended in Genesis, in Jesus, God has done just that.

The first feature of being our Way-Maker is what Jesus leads us out of and away from. The second feature of Jesus our Way-Maker is what he leads us into. When John says, "There is one coming after me who is mightier than me" , John reminds us that Jesus is the one who can solve our problem of how to be righteous before God (Matthew 3:11, KJV). John baptized with water, but Jesus baptizes with the Holy Spirit and fire. Jesus has our back. He covers for us.

When I was a boy raised on the farm, we always had chores. Some, I could handle. Some, I wasn't that good at doing. The good news is that my daddy would come behind me and "check" my work. Yes, he would give encouragement and correction, but by the time he was through, the job was done perfectly.

When Jesus makes a way for us, he does the same thing. That is good news. Jesus, who is the righteous one, died that he might bring us to God. The promise inherent in Jesus being the Way-Maker is that he will not only go ahead of us—lay his life down for our redemption—but will also come behind us in the power of the Holy Spirit to present us before the throne of God without spot or blemish, totally righteous.

The third aspect of Jesus as the Way-Maker is what he leads us through. The hymn "Where He Leads, I Will Follow" says it this way: "I'll go with him through the judgment. I'll go with him all the way." The way Jesus provides has the approval of God. "This is my beloved Son in whom I am well pleased" (Matthew 3:17, KJV). Isaiah 53:10 says, "It pleased God to crush him and cause him to suffer, and though the Lord makes his life a guilt offering, he will see his offspring and prolong his days and the will of the Lord will prosper in his hand."

God has chosen. It's our turn. "Whoever believes in him (Jesus) is not condemned, but whoever does not believe stands condemned already because he has not believed in the name of God's one and only Son" (John 3:18).

Jesus Gives Salvation

How does God do this? Ephesians 1 says that God eulogizes us even while we are yet dead in sin. In Christ Jesus, we who have nothing or any power to change our status before God have it changed for us. We are blessed with all spiritual blessings in Jesus. God gives salvation. It is based on God's foreknowledge—God's ability to see us in his Son. God does not see us as unable to change. "By grace we are saved through faith. It is the gift of God" (Ephesians 2:8).

It is only by looking at each other the way God does (in faith) that we can hope for a better future. By those who know me best, I am judged by my past. They might want what is best for me, but they cannot escape what they know about me. My future is limited and confined by my past. Even if I change my behavior for the best, it will hold a temporary status until faith is applied.

At one church I served there was a wife who came to me concerned about her husband. She said, "I don't know what to do with him. Could you talk to him and see if you could help?" The young man had a history of drinking and doing drugs. The effect of these addictions had caught up with him and his relationship with his wife. He also had an injured back, which contributed to the problem.

We talked, and I agreed to provide transportation each morning to the hospital and back for counseling. The days passed, and I could begin to see a change in him. I encouraged him to seek the face of Jesus to satisfy his appetite for life instead of the drugs and alcohol. We prayed together for his healing.

He was healed. He became a faithful man. He offered his talents to the church and began to lead the music in worship. It wasn't long before his wife called again saying, "I don't know what to do with him. He's here all the time and trying to be helpful. Can you talk to him and see if you could help?" I told her I would come and talk with her instead.

I subsequently told his mother and his wife they would have to raise their level of faith to help maintain his. Hadn't their prayers been answered? Hadn't salvation come to their house?

Zechariah was given a prophetic picture of the ministry of the Messiah. His soon-to-be-born son, John, would announce the Messiah's coming. Every person's faith would rise and fall in relationship to the Messiah. Jesus is the Messiah. God has chosen Jesus to be the chief cornerstone of God's salvation plan. Jesus is the Truth and Life that brings us into God's new creation.

Jesus Untangles Us from Our Sin

God knows it doesn't do us any good to know what's right and not be able to do it. Actually, those who know better are more accountable than those who are ignorant. This is why God continues to give good news. Jesus untangles or delivers us from our sin. Salvation is a gift, and the promise of Jesus being the one who untangles us from our sin means the gift can be unwrapped and enjoyed.

Plant something. It will never be as beautiful or fruitful as you want it to be if the ground is never cultivated. Weeds and thorns will choke the life out of what has been planted. Likewise, salvation is a gift, but it is a gift that must be cultivated. We are able to grow and become fruitful as God nurtures the gift within our lives.

Watch Jesus as he is led by the Spirit, fed by the word of God, and renewed in prayer and obedience. He walks the same pathway we are called to follow. Our faith will be built up and flourish following the example of Jesus.

He Is Tender Mercy Incarnate

A teacher once said, "God saves those who are bound, but he only serves through those who are free." Jesus said, "For even the Son of Man did not come to be served, but to serve, and to give his life as a ransom for many" (Mark 10:45). Jesus' offering was a willing sacrifice and not a grudging obligation. Mercy does not operate out of obligation but out of love. "God so loved the world that he gave his only begotten Son, that whosoever believes in him will not perish but have everlasting life" (John 3:16). Jesus expresses the love of God substantially. He chooses in the garden of Gethsemane to say, "Yet, not my will, but yours be done" (Luke 22:42b). Jesus chooses to offer himself as tender mercy incarnate so that we might have something definite to which to respond.

The choice of Jesus calls for you and me to make a choice. Will we love and trust Jesus? Will we allow his substantial choice to make a substantial difference in us? I preached a sermon in my first pastoral appointment on loving others in this substantial way. An older lady chided me afterwards about the necessity of preaching what I did. She asked, "Preacher, don't you know I love everybody?" I very naively and tactlessly replied, "That's good, but I want to know if you love anybody in particular."

Jesus was very particular how he loved us.

He Inspects Us for Approval

Jesus looks us square in the eye, knows our heart, and gives to each of us the choice between life and death. Who else can walk by while we are busy living and say, "Follow me"? Who else can look at us as Jesus looked at Peter and say, "Don't be afraid; from now on you will catch men" (Luke 5:10)? Who but Jesus can command us to move forward in life and sin no more? Who can require so much that we have to decide between leaving them or loving them? In John 6:66–68, many had come to this place of decision. Thousands of those following Jesus at the time walked away from Jesus. A few decided to walk with him. Jesus asked, "You do not want to leave, too, do you?" (v. 67). Simon Peter answered, "Lord, to whom shall we go? You have the words of eternal life. We believe and know you are the Holy One of God" (vv. 68–69).

Have you realized, as Peter did, who Jesus is? Have you made your choice to follow him? Only those who freely follow are sent by Jesus to serve the world. Everybody else is just playing their own game, following their own drummer. Is your life marked by Jesus' approval? Has he inspected your heart and said, "You're good to go"?

He Guides Us in the Way of Peace

How would you rate your relationships? If you are married, how would you rate your marriage on a scale of one to ten? The number one represents a marriage filled with dissention, and the number ten is a marriage where everything clicks. The way of peace is the way that clicks. This is Jesus. He is the Prince of Peace. You could paraphrase Jesus' ministry as "I and the Father are one."

Think about it. Can you imagine Jesus ever saying, "I wish I hadn't done that," or "Whoa, that was way out of line."? No, the way of Jesus, the way of peace, is a way of no regrets because it is the way of salvation.

The way of peace is the way of constant connectivity to God. This way is not easy and does not come naturally to us. We must lean forward as we walk and try to catch every word our Savior says. We have God's promise that as we draw near to him, God will draw near to us. Jesus, our guide in the way of peace, shares the indwelling Holy Spirit with us. By the Spirit, we have all we need, everything that pertains to life and godliness.

So let us walk in the way of peace. "Let us throw off everything that hinders and the sin that so easily entangles, and let us run with perseverance the race marked out for us. Let us fix our eyes on Jesus" (Hebrews 12:1b–2a). Jesus has even thrown off the grip of death, so you might freely follow the pathway of grace. Go ahead. What are you waiting for?

JESUS: OUR POINT OF REFERENCE

All the promises in the world would do us no good if they could not be put into practice. The good news is that Jesus is the Great Practitioner. He demonstrates and embodies the pathway we are meant to follow. Jesus literally had his faith tested. Reading the scriptures, we can see him actually exchange temptation for the word of God. We can tell the difference between those who have trusted in his saving work and those who haven't.

We can observe Jesus' anointed, prayer-filled life. His ministry is a historical fact. Jesus is tender mercy incarnate. John 1:14 says, "The Word became flesh and made his dwelling among us. We have seen his glory, the glory of the One and Only, who came from the Father, full of grace and truth."

You can make a movie that displays his passion. It would take more than our lifetime to share the testimony of those whose lives have been changed by his resurrection and the way of peace Jesus provides.

Yes, Jesus not only gets our hopes up, he is our blessed hope! Jesus is the one who walks the pathway of grace and calls us to follow. His whole life was a perfect picture of the path we should follow. The remaining sections in this chapter include different ways Jesus provides a point of reference as we follow the pathway of God's grace.

In His Baptism

When Jesus comes to John to be baptized in the Jordan, Jesus is beginning the pathway of grace. Jesus begins this journey, as we must, in repentance. But Jesus had no sin to confess. He had no wrong that needed forgiving. What Jesus did come to do was to make a new start. Jesus is the Way-Maker, and he came to baptism to represent the will of the Father for all of humanity. John understands that Jesus does not come to baptism to repent of sin. Matthew 3:14–15 tells us, "John tried to deter him, saying, 'I need to be baptized by you, and do you come to me?' Jesus replied, 'Let it be so now; it is proper for us to do this to fulfill all righteousness.' Then John consented."

Jesus is claiming to represent the repentance of God. God is making a new covenant. Hebrews 1:1–2a says, "In the past God spoke to our forefathers through the prophets at many times and in various ways, but in these last days he has spoken to us by his Son." So with this new covenant, God's judgment hasn't changed. God is still judging our hearts by faith.

In the baptism of Jesus, God sharpens and gives focus to our faith. God makes it personal. "This is my beloved Son in whom I am well pleased" (Matthew 3:17, KJV).

In the beginning, the standard was set when the command was given: "And the Lord God commanded the man, 'You are free to eat from any tree in the garden; but you must not eat from the tree of the knowledge of good and evil, for when you eat of it you will surely die'" (Genesis 2:16–17). The transgression of that commandment by our first parents has had deadly results. Sin and its consequences are in our DNA. Yet, from the very beginning a sacrifice was made to cover or atone for that sin.

One command eventually gave way to whole systems of law and moral codes. All these multiplied transgressions and served to put us all under the same judgment: "The soul that sins, it shall die" (Ezekiel 18:20). The good news is that I am not held responsible for the guilt of anyone but myself. The bad news is that I need a new heart and a new spirit if I am to live a life that is upright and not guilty before God. What can cover for me when I don't fulfill God's perfect will? Thankfully, Jesus can and will. He says so when he comes to his baptism.

We still need a new heart and a new spirit. But God, through the testimony of John, also declares Jesus will keep us covered by being the One who will baptize us in the Holy Spirit. Jesus, the Bread from Heaven, will feed us and supply us with what we need.

In the beginning, it was plain. God says, "If you eat of the fruit of the tree of the knowledge of good and evil, you will die" (Genesis 2:17). Now, Jesus makes it equally plain:

> I tell you the truth, unless you eat the flesh of the Son of Man and drink his blood, you have no life in you. Whoever eats my flesh and drinks my blood has eternal life, and I will raise him up at the last day. For my flesh is real food and my blood is real drink. Whoever eats my flesh and drinks my blood remains in me, and I in him. Just as the living Father sent me and I live because of the Father, so the one who feeds on me will live because of me.
>
> John 6:53–58

Jesus is the Way-Maker. Jesus initiates that way in his baptism, representing the Father, fulfilling all righteousness. It's no wonder that followers of the way still come to be baptized into Jesus and share in communion with him.

In the Wilderness Testing

Jesus gives source and substance to God's salvation. It is in dependence upon God and his word. During baptism, Jesus manifests God's salvation by receiving the affirmation of the Father. How do you know you are saved? You know it the same way Jesus did. God says so, and you believe. How do you know you are being saved? In fasting and prayer, seemingly living without anything, you find out God is the source of all you need. When temptation comes that questions who you are, you define yourself by the singular voice of Spirit-breathed scripture. When you are asked to define yourself by your appetites or by what is rational, instead you affirm what the word of God says about you. When you are asked to define yourself by your sense of justice or idealism, instead you affirm what the word of God says about you. When you are asked to define yourself by power or powerlessness, instead you affirm what the word of God says about you.

Salvation finds its victory in the faith of Jesus. It is Jesus who demonstrates in the wilderness testing that even if we come to a place of total depravity, God will provide us strength and provision.

In the Anointing of the Holy Spirit

What does it mean that Jesus moved in the anointing of the Holy Spirit? First, the anointing pointed to his authority to act as prophet, priest, and king. More than that, it meant there was no halfway with Jesus. He was 100 percent human. He was 100 percent divine. "The fullness of the deity dwelt in him bodily" (Colossians 2:9).

Second, moving within the anointing of the Holy Spirit meant that Jesus was not just appropriate most of the time. Jesus was always appropriate. In that anointing Jesus followed the pathway of grace. Luke 4 describes it this way. Jesus is anointed:

- To preach good news to the poor
- To heal the brokenhearted
- To proclaim freedom to the captives
- The recovery of sight to the blind
- To restore those who are crushed
- To proclaim the acceptable year of the Lord

So then, for those who are helpless and hopeless, Jesus is the embodiment of good news. He makes a way when there is no way.

Jesus begins in the place that scares us, the gulf between where we are and where we need to be. He gives us a pro for our every con. In addition, when Jesus heals what's broken, he has us wrapped tightly in his care. Even if we come unglued, we are okay: "He upholds everything with the word of his power" (Hebrew 1:3). The Roman centurion in Luke 7 realized what this meant (Luke 7:1–10). Listen to the key phrase offered to Jesus by the centurion. "But say the word, and my servant will be healed. For I myself am a man under authority" (vv. 7–8). All the fruit of the Spirit, including healing, are the result of being under the authority of the anointing.

Jesus also brings freedom to the captives. Captive here denotes a perfectly fit and capable person who has been speared or captured and is now a prisoner of war. They are under restraints and all their strength and attributes are of no use to them. Within the anointing, those restraints are removed. So consider the anointing as its own best recommendation. To choose doing your best over doing everything under the anointing is like choosing Richard Simmons instead of Tony Horton of P90X to be your personal trainer. So much more is possible under the anointing of God. The following two stories are examples. The first story is mundane, the other quite extraordinary.

Our mission team was in Brazil and had formed a prayer tunnel, two members of the team facing each other and praying for the person passing between them. Betty McKinney and I were at the end of the line. As we touched and prayed for each person, there was a clarity and confidence for what we ought to pray. When I felt led to be quiet, Betty was already praying. When Betty remained quiet, I was praying. When we both prayed, we quoted each other.

The more extraordinary incident of operating under the anointing took place in 2003 during "The World's Longest Sermon," a world record attempt to make the gospel of Jesus as unavoidable as possible. The sermon began at 6:00 a.m. on Friday, and I finished at 11:05 a.m. Sunday. It was the wee hours of the morning on Sunday. I was mentally and physically exhausted. Though I had three separate notebooks I used to guide my preaching, I thought I was repeating myself. Because I was so tired I was getting confused and disoriented.

That's when the questions started. Different people in the congregation began to ask me questions about the scripture. I began to respond. There was a crowd of about thirty-five there, and each one, it seemed, had a different question about what the scripture was saying. I got revved up and excited. My energy level was renewed, and I was able to make it through the rest of the night.

At the mandatory fifteen-minute break that came Sunday morning, I thanked everyone for their questions and told them how much I appreciated them. A member of my church, Todd Peters, responded to me. He said, "Norm, we didn't ask you any questions, but you did answer everything I was thinking about."

This incident shows that we do not have to be consciously aware of the Spirit's anointing for it to cover us in a remarkable way. I trust that these stories illustrate the importance of the anointing governing all we do. Each time the anointing governs our activity, it puts us in the right place with other people. It puts us in the place of agreement, the place of power. The anointing serves as an umbrella for discernment and discovery. This is why the anointing set the course for Jesus' public ministry. This is why Jesus can announce the acceptable year of the Lord. Anytime you walk into a situation or environment under the anointing, it becomes a place of decision, a place where in that given time and place salvation can come.

In His Public Ministry

Jesus traveled lightly. He only did what he saw the Father doing. The anointing of the Holy Spirit was the only thing he needed to carry. That's why you never saw him overwhelmed with the enormity of need. Yes, he got tired. Yes, a lot of demands were made upon him. But Jesus was always able to meet the core need of people and move in obedience to the Father's direction, whether it was speaking to a single Samaritan woman or feeding five thousand.

Peter describes Jesus in Acts 10:37–38 this way: "You know what has happened throughout Judea, beginning in Galilee after the baptism that John preached—how God anointed Jesus of Nazareth with the Holy Spirit and power, and how he went around doing good and healing all who were under the power of the devil, because God was with him."

Jesus walked through Galilee and Judea because that's what he was sent to do. His ministry had two main goals, according to Peter. The first goal was to reveal the glory or *good* of God. The second was to exchange the power and dominion exercised over people by the devil for the dominion exercised for their good by God. Jesus was the mediator for that exchange. Through repentance and faith in Jesus, the kingdom of God drew near and was manifested in the lives of ordinary people.

In His Passion

In his passion Jesus broke down every barrier between God and us. The blood of Jesus not only satisfied the ancient demands of the law of sin and death, the blood created a new law: the law of the Spirit of life! Through the passion of Jesus, this new law created the ultimate paradigm shift. Instead of hostility between you and God, there can now be peace. Instead of endless replays of try, try again, you can now achieve and appreciate the strength and goodness of God.

When I was in college, I had a religion professor named Dr. James E. Hull. Dr. Hull always had faith in me. When the scholarship I had ended after my freshman year, I did not know how I would continue my education. Dr. Hull knew. He went to various groups unbeknownst to me and raised the money to match and then exceed my former scholarship. All that was required for me to receive it was the promise of future service in ministry. God had already called me to the ministry by then, so it was no problem for me to say I would serve. My intentions and commitments to serve, though, wouldn't have amounted to anything without the scholarship.

The passion of Jesus works the same way for us. It gives us everything. All of our intentions and commitments to serve don't mean anything apart from his passion. Yet, receiving the gifts and benefits of Jesus' passion makes serving and sharing life with God not only possible but also a reality.

In His Resurrection

I used to follow Interstate 77, the West Virginia Turnpike, when I went to seminary. Back then I went through the Memorial Tunnel that went under Paint Creek Mountain. In 1987, they finished the massive road-cutting project that bypassed the tunnel and the Bender Bridge. The old way was cut off.

The same thing has happened in the way our soul is saved and brought to life. The old ways have been set aside. Hebrews 10 says that Jesus has opened and dedicated a new and living way into the Most Holy Place through his own body and blood. Everything else—balancing the scales of good and evil, fulfilling the law, offering sacrifices, becoming spiritual—is now a road to nowhere.

It is God's great act of breakthrough—the resurrection of Jesus from the dead—that commands our hearts to quit wasting our time and energy on the wrong road and to instead travel well the pathway of grace. Jesus tells us where to start in the first words of his ministry: "Repent and believe for the kingdom of God is near" (Mark 1:15). Peter echoes the same message when hearts were stirred up on the day of Pentecost. They asked, "Now that we know that God has raised Jesus from the dead, what shall we do?" The answer: "Repent and be baptized, every one of you, in the name of Jesus Christ for the forgiveness of sins. And you will receive the gift of the Holy Spirit" (Acts 2:38).

Paul affirms this truth in Athens where every way and philosophy was being bandied about. "In the past God overlooked such ignorance, but now he commands all people everywhere to repent. For he has set a day when he will judge the world with justice by the man he has appointed. He has given proof of this to all men by raising him from the dead" (Acts 17:30–31).

It's time for you to answer God's call upon your life. It's time to respond seriously to the claims of Jesus. Everything is now judged in light of our path finding its completion in Jesus. The resurrection of Jesus blares: "There are no other detours! The straight way is finished and open. It is time for you to be moving at the speed of grace!"

SMALL GROUP
DISCUSSION QUESTIONS

1. In the past, what has been your point of origin for your spiritual life? Have you started at the right point, or has it been more of a self-improvement journey?

2. Can you see that Jesus needs to be our point of origin if we are going to grow in our spiritual relationship with God? If so, why?

3. How can knowing Jesus' walk on this earth help you to grow with God?

4. Which part of Jesus' life do you need to know better to help your walk on the pathway of grace? His baptism? His testing? His anointing? His ministry? His passion? His resurrection? How do you need to open your life, so Jesus can work in you?

Begin in Repentance

After John was put in prison, Jesus went into Galilee, proclaiming the good news of God. "The time has come," he said. "The kingdom of God is near. Repent and believe the good news."

Mark 1:14–15

God was reconciling the world to himself in Christ, not counting men's sins against them. And he has committed to us the message of reconciliation. We are therefore Christ's ambassadors, as though God were making his appeal through us. We implore you on Christ's behalf: Be reconciled to God.

2 Corinthians 5:19–20

Whatever you may be sure of, be sure of this: that you are dreadfully like other people.

—Robert Frost

THE BEGINNING OF OUR JOURNEY

There are many examples of the path God follows in our lives. As we saw in the introduction, tying shoes is just one. The life cycle of a farmer is another illustration of how God works in the world. In the beginning the farmer prepares the soil, aligning the character of the soil to best suit what he desires to plant. Then, he plants the seed. What's planted is cultivated, watered, and tended. The farmer gathers in the harvest for the benefit of himself and others. He markets that crop, and to perpetuate this cycle of life, he saves some of his seed for the next season.

The Bible says that from the beginning, the creation witnesses to God's eternal power and his divinity so that we are all without excuse. Romans 8:28 says the whole of creation works under the orchestration of God for our good.

The scripture is wonderful in how it reinforces its own truth. Romans 8:28–30 lays out the pattern of God's movement in our lives and then verses 31–39 restate that pattern from a different angle. It reminds us that God calls us because God is for us. God foreknows us, so he alone can give us all that we need in life. God has predestined us to be conformed into the image of his Son, so he alone can make an evaluation of our life. Righteousness originates in God.

God calls us again and is interceding for us. He lives so that we might attain and secure the life we were meant to live. Apart from God we can do nothing. Abiding within his intercession we can do all things. He alone justifies us. We are more than conquerors, revelations of God's passion and resurrection. Nothing can separate us from the love of God in Christ Jesus. God's work will be complete when we are glorified with him.

"What then shall we say to these things?" (Romans 8:31). If this is the way God works, then this is the way I want to work. If this is the pattern of movement God follows, then I will become a disciple and move with him. Practically, this may mean for some you need to be baptized, aligning yourselves with the way, the truth, and the life that is Jesus. You need to confess Jesus as Lord with your own lips. Do you need to find a place to belong with those who share this same faith? Do you need to exercise yourself in ministry, led by the Holy Spirit? Do you need to become a sign of Christ's passion, his salt and light? Do you need to share in the power of his resurrection, to live in anticipation of the soon coming of Christ our King? Begin in repentance.

What Does Repentance Mean?

The word *repentance* comes from a Greek word *metanoia,* which simply means with our minds. Most of the time when the scripture calls for repentance it speaks of our mind turning to God. Paul celebrates this change when he writes to the church in Thessalonica, praising them for turning from idols to serve the living and the true God.

First, repentance implies accompaniment. It means we are going to follow somebody or something that we haven't followed up to now. I have learned in my life that the way to move forward is to find somebody that is ahead of you. Find somebody who knows something you don't, and spend some time with that person. Find a mentor, coach, or teacher who knows something that you don't. Move forward, and try to catch up to your mentor.

Repentance means, then, to accompany Jesus wherever he goes. We commit to a relationship of friendship with God through Jesus Christ. Jesus walks the pathway of grace, and so we begin to walk it with him. We begin to acknowledge our betrayal, acknowledge where we have fallen short of God's glory in our lives or the way that God wants us to live. We turn from the ways we have been deceived and the lies that we have believed. These may be ways that we have failed to do what we knew we were supposed to do, or things we did that we knew we shouldn't have done. These may be lies about ourselves or lies others have told us. Nevertheless, we acknowledge these failings and begin to accompany Jesus into our new life.

Second, not only does repentance imply a sense of accompaniment, but it also means we align ourselves with God as opposed to our own way or following a way set by others. Jesus says, "Wide is the path that leads to destruction. Many go that way, but the way that leads to life is narrow and straight. Few there are that find it" (Matthew 7:13–14, paraphrase). We have to align ourselves precisely and correctly with God to do that. Jesus said in order to find that way we must be born again. We must be born from above. God must do something—regenerate the hope of life in us so that we can follow him. *Say this prayer right now:* "God, bring the regenerative power of your grace to bear in my life. I want to align myself with you."

Alignment is usually translated by using the word *submission*. We shy away from that word, but it is the same word that we would use for car maintenance. We take our car to the shop and have our tires lined up so that they don't wear out unevenly or pull us off into the ditch because they are out of alignment.

Do not be threatened or made fearful by the word *submission*. We submit ourselves to the Lord because as the Lord walks the way, we walk it with him. We are aligning ourselves with God and the words that he says, the advice that he gives, and the power that he bestows. The Bible says as many as receive Jesus, to them he gives power to become sons of God. The Bible is also filled with examples of repentance. We see repentance in the Bible when people came to Jesus and asked him to have mercy on them. We see repentance when the disciples decide to leave their boats and follow Jesus.

So, what happens when we align ourselves? When we align ourselves, we each say, "God I want access to all that I need. I want to reverence you. I want to worship you. I want to put myself where I am humble before you, submitted to you. I kneel down to you. My will, my heart, my strength, and my soul; everything is yours."

Third, repentance is also embracing and holding onto the

vision that God has for your life. No longer are we iden*
betrayal or by our own way, but by God's vision for u
Peter and his brothers, "I will make you fishers of mei
4:19). He says to us, "I will make you who you were always meant to
be. I will not leave you comfortless. I will not leave you as orphans,
but I will come to you and I will make you who you are supposed to
be. I will love you into the person you are to become."

Turn to God and repent. Don't put that off. What keeps you
from turning to God? There is no line in which you have to wait.
There are no hoops to jump through. There is not a single requirement that hasn't already been fulfilled. Because of the blood of
Jesus, because of God's own choice, the way has been paved for you
to follow.

Suppose you have been working on your computer and you
need software to make it more efficient, to keep it from freezing
up and crashing. You find the site that will transform your computer and solve your problems. You're willing to pay big time for
its promised results. When you land on the site, you find out the
solution is a free download if you agree to its terms of use. You don't
even read the terms. Your need is so great; you're so tired of your
computer locking up, you immediately check the box "I accept" and
move toward getting the software downloaded into your computer.
You admit your need. You accept the terms of use. You access the
software and download it. You act on the promise of what it will do.

Jesus asks us to do the same thing. Some hesitate and say they
don't understand how God will work. We don't know how our computer works either, but we trust it and use it anyway. What happens
then, that we don't respond immediately to the call of Jesus? The
terms of use are easy to understand. Proverbs 16:6 says, "By mercy
and truth iniquity is purged and by the fear of the Lord a man
departs from evil." So repentance is a departing—a departing from
evil and a departing from our way. It involves us receiving what
God wants to give and departing from what God wants to remove
from our life. Can we come to God, receive what God wants to
give, and not turn away from what God wants us to remove? Not

really. We can't accompany somebody unless we leave something else. This turning is premeditated since it involves our will and our ability to freely choose. God is asking us today to accompany him, align ourselves with his kingdom, and accept his Son as our Lord and Savior.

Fourth, repentance involves mercy and truth. Notice particularly the dual application of these words regarding our sin in Proverbs 16:6. Sometimes we get off balance and want to receive mercy only; however, mercy without truth will lead us to be spoiled. It will lead us to have a spirit of entitlement when it comes to God. We won't come to God as little children but as bitter, demanding adults. We will be victims that need to find the wrong kind of satisfaction in God.

God is not going to deal with us that way. We don't come to God on this basis: "If you had done a better job, God, I wouldn't have been in this mess." That doesn't work. We don't come spoiled and get what we want. My children were taught very early that you don't get anything by whining, grumbling, and complaining. It just doesn't work that way. Mercy is not ever divided from truth. Truth is never divided from mercy. If it were, it would be a legalistic nightmare. God doesn't give me what I deserve. (Thank you, Lord.)

I have heard it said that if we were the only ones alive, God loved us so much he would have sent Jesus to die for us, just us. I believe God's love is that great. But if that sentiment is not expressed in humility, in mercy mixed with truth, then we might as well say, "If somebody has to die, I don't want it to be me. Kill your son. Don't do anything with me. Just put it on him."

The truth is, God did lay on Jesus the iniquity of us all. The truth is, we deserved the death Jesus suffered for us. But, the truth is, Jesus died as an expression of God's mercy and goodness. The goodness of God, the book of Romans tells us, is designed and given to lead us to repentance. In this last section we will explore further the importance of repentance.

Why Is Repentance Necessary?

Why is repentance so important? We cannot begin any other way. Without repentance, everything else we do is a dead work. We're still running the show, out of place, running on a virtual, parallel track. There is a wall that still stands between God and us. It may be see-through, but it still disconnects us from the thoroughfare of God's grace. Suppose we come to the end of our lives and have accomplished great exploits of faith, become very wise, and have blessed and influenced others, but we never began in repentance. All will amount to nothing without repentance and alignment with God.

Alignment, then, is an act of love. God loves us and asks for our love in return. He asks for our heart. "'Give me thy heart,' says the Father above. No gift so precious to Him as our love" (Bowen, 1938, 129). We give God our heart so that we can do all of these other things.

Repentance is necessary because without it everything else is dead. The one thing God must have is the surrender of our heart. Everything else is just a mockery. It is a sham.

Another reason why repentance must occur is because Jesus said we must be born again to enter into the kingdom of heaven. We must turn to God in repentance and in love to enter into the kingdom of heaven. Some will argue, "No, I am a child of God. I am made in God's image." Just because we were made in God's image, and we have the possibility of living with God in a unity of spirit, soul, and body does not now give us access into the kingdom.

When we went on vacation recently, we were issued room keys, and they were made in the image of all the other room keys. They all looked the same, but I found that I could only open my door with the keys I had been given. I could not open anybody else's doors, and I am thankful because that meant other people couldn't open my door either. You had to have authorization. You had to have the codes written into your key to get in. It didn't matter that your key was made in the image of all of the other keys. It didn't matter that it shared their likeness. To have access into my room, you had to have it coded a certain way. Jesus said it works the same way in his kingdom. Just because you're made in his image doesn't mean you're authorized to come in. You must be born again, and that begins with repentance.

I had a friend one time who was concerned about her father. He had had an "after death experience." I know you have heard of those where people die, and they see the light or go through the tunnel into the light. He had had that experience and felt this great warmth and felt like "Wow! This is a great place to come." He was resuscitated and brought back to this life again.

The reason why his daughter came to me was because she was concerned. She said that before he had this experience, he didn't want to have anything to do with God or Jesus, and he didn't care about heaven or anything else. Now only one thing had changed. He wanted to get back to that place, but he still didn't care anything about God or Jesus.

"What can I do? What can I tell him?" she asked.

I directed her attention to a parable about "The Great Supper," the great banquet feast. The guests are all there and the Lord of the dinner comes in and notices someone is there who doesn't have a robe of righteousness on. It was like "How did you get in here? Where is your robe?" The guest was speechless. He didn't know about this robe thing. He didn't have an answer. He was thrown out and cast out into outer darkness where there was weeping and wailing and gnashing of teeth.

I told her to share this story with her father and to explain that not everybody that gets into the party gets to stay for the party. That is true. God has given all of us an invitation, but if we get into the party or crash the party, if we are wedding crashers and the Lord of the wedding spots us (and he will), we won't get to stay.

This parable and my friend's story illustrate why repentance is so important. This is why you can't begin any other way. You cannot jump directly from walking the path of sin to doing what you want to do on the pathway of grace. In some ways the two paths correspond to each other. There is a way that beginning in repentance corresponds to our betrayal. There is a way that believing in the Lord Jesus corresponds to the bias that we can have, the blindness we can have in our souls. Blame assigns responsibility, but not in the same direction as building up our faith does. The bitter person wants to make things better, but their results are different from those who are led by the Spirit to bless. While these parallels exist, one of the worst mistakes we can make is to think we can just jump track, bypassing repentance. Your root determines your fruit. Observe a bitter person. They say, "All I want to do is help people. All I want to do is bless people. I have been hurt so much in my life that I just want to do what's good."

They begin to do good, and what happens? Everybody feels and receives every good thing they want to do as an act of bitterness. Jesus said if you want the fruit (or the results) to be good, the tree has to be good (Matthew 12:33). That is why John the Baptist, the prophet who called people to repentance, said the same thing. "The ax is already at the root of the trees and every tree that does not produce good fruit will be cut down and thrown into the fire" (Matthew 3:10).

You can't jump track. You can't just jump in and crash the wedding or crash the party and expect to stay. That is why repentance is absolutely necessary. Without it you will overexpose mercy to ignore the truth or lift up truth and strangle mercy. Without repentance everything else you do will end up being dead. It will end up giving you the illusion that you can get into the party without it and that you will be the exception that gets to stay.

I saw how this worked when I was in seminary. I was an early riser. I got up early in the morning happy and thankful for the day ahead. I took my joy with me when I went across the hall to get my shower. As I showered I would sing my thanks and praise to God. Meanwhile, my friend whose room was next door to the shower, who was not an early riser, found my singing did not bring him the same joy. (And I have a good voice.) No, my friend found my singing altogether unpleasant and left a scripture verse on my door to let me know. "If a man loudly blesses his neighbor early in the morning, it will be taken as a curse" (Proverbs 27:14).

I quit singing in the shower after that. Why? Isn't it obvious? My singing was rooted more in my lack of concern for my neighbor than my love for God. I still sang, just at more appropriate times and places.

God says, "I need your heart, give me your heart." Jesus says, "The greatest thing you can do is love the Lord your God with all your heart, soul, mind and strength" (Luke 10:27). That begins in repentance. Repentance is just one step on the path of grace. It is the first step. You will come back to it over and over again, but from now on you'll come back by going forward. You're going to move forward toward it through faith in Jesus Christ. You'll strengthen your faith. Apply it to life. You'll become a trailblazer. When you breakthrough into newness of life, it will lead you into new dimensions of repentance.

SMALL GROUP DISCUSSION QUESTIONS

1. Do you see repentance in a new light after reading this chapter?

2. Take some time to examine your life. What areas of your life need the light of truth, so you can experience God's mercy in its fullness?

3. Think about the fact that repentance means departing or turning from sin. What do you need to turn away from for your spiritual life to grow? What do you need to turn toward to better walk in the way of grace?

4. Spend some time with God talking about repentance. Report to your group about the items you are willing to turn from and what you are seeking to turn to at this time in your spiritual journey.

"Let this mind be in you, which was also in Christ Jesus" (Philippians 2:5, KJV).

SHARING THE MINDSET OF JESUS

As I said in chapter 2, repentance literally means with our mind. If our thoughts create our life, then repentance is where our life of faith in God is created. Repentance is the first manifestation of faith—the nexus between God's heart and ours.

Repentance is not just an admission that we're a mess and we need changing, but that God is good and if we are to do the works of God, our minds and hearts must change direction. We must go with God. Jesus says, "Come and see," and we head off in the direction he is going. We accompany Jesus.

What is the goal of repentance? Is it to be at peace with God? Is it to share the mind of Christ? Is it to receive and possess the unconscious ability to love? Is it to find ourselves as soul mates of Jesus? Is it to become a friend of God? Yes. Yes. Yes. Yes and yes. The goal of repentance, the realization of moving at the speed of grace, is to do all these things. It is to exercise our minds as Jesus does. It is to be mentally predisposed to follow and obey the word of God!

Can we develop such a mindset? Can we find ourselves in a relationship with God like I observed in my grandfather and grandmother? They were married for sixty-three years. They complemented each other so well, uniquely different, yet one. They were very different in how their minds operated, but they could complete each other's sentences. They were equals. They even looked more and more like each other as they grew older together. But you would never mistake one for the other.

This is the relationship God initiates in repentance. It is a life where I give praise and honor to God as he shares his favor and pleasure with me. Uniquely different, yet one, we are drawn together through the blood of Jesus Christ.

We are equals. "His divine power has given us everything we need for life and godliness through our knowledge of him who called us by his own glory and goodness. Through these he has given us his very great and precious promises, so that through them you may participate in the divine nature and escape the corruption in the world caused by evil desires" (2 Peter 1:3). Yes, we are equals. We look more and more like each other as we grow, but you would never mistake one for the other.

Don't get mad at me here. I am not trying to be a heretic or some new age guru. When I speak of equality with God, I never mean that when all is said and done, you won't be able to tell God and me apart. I am speaking in human terms that God is an equal opportunity grace giver. Romans 5:1–2 says that when God justifies us, we are given free and total access to God's grace.

Equal access, equal opportunity does not mean the same or equal outcomes. Michael Phelps and I may have equal access into a public pool, but if you ask me who can go from one end to the other quicker, I'm going to bet he can.

Listen to this. "For this is what the high and lofty One says— he who lives forever, whose name is holy: 'I live in a high and holy place, but also with him who is contrite and lowly in spirit, to revive the spirit of the lowly and to revive the heart of the contrite'" (Isaiah 57:15). The humble and the holy can occupy the same space. The lofty One and the lowly one can move along together. How is this pursuit enabled? How is this mental disposition developed? It is by following the pathway of God's grace. Philippians 2:5 says, "Let this mind be in you which was also in Christ Jesus." As the Apostle Paul conveys the portrait of Jesus' mind, we examine Philippians 2:6–8 for the steps useful for the development of our own mindset.

"Who Did Not Think Equality with God Was Something to Be Grasped ..."

Equality with God is not something to be grasped.
It is not a right or entitlement.
It is not something we deserve or earn.
It is not something that can be bargained for.

It cannot be seized or obtained.

It is a gift to be received. "It is the gift of God, not of works, lest any man should boast" (Ephesians 2:8–9, KJV).

Equality with God is not something granted to us because we occupy time and space. It doesn't matter that we're matter. It is not a gift of the universe or the cosmos. We are not after some knockoff of what God can give. We're after the oneness and unity that Jesus prayed we would have.

We all would like a life of breakthrough. We all want to bring life (of some variety) and make a difference in the world. We all want to bless others. We all want to build up our faith, justify our existence. We all want to believe we are living a good life or as good as we can make it for ourselves.

The call to repentance reminds us we all have to begin that making somewhere. The call to repentance says we do not have to go it alone. The call to repentance affirms that life can be fully enjoyed and experienced in relationship with God. There doesn't have to be a rivalry between us. Equality with God that has to be grasped is trying to marry your rival.

Karen and I have been married over twenty-one years. I am male. She is female. I grew up in one place for the better part of my life. She has averaged moving about every eighteen months. She grew up in town and in the city. I grew up in the country.

Once upon a time we attended a seminar together. We were given a questionnaire. The questions evaluated how we approached different situations. Thirty-six scenarios were presented and used to judge how we would respond. These scenarios ran the gamut from a one-on-one conversation, to settling a group argument, to speaking before a large audience.

When we came into the room where the counselor would interpret our results, there was a look of concern on his face.

"Are y'all alright?" he began.

Karen and I looked at each other and said, "Yeah."

"Are you sure?" he replied.

"Yes," we assured him. We were fine; not perfect, but okay. We asked him what was wrong.

He said he had never seen anything like it before in all his years of practice. *Hadn't seen what?* we thought. "Are you sure you're okay?" he asked again. "You aren't arguing or fighting all the time?"

We were getting confused. "No," we said again. We rarely fight. We enjoy each other and have a lot of fun together. Finally, we said "We're married. We love each other."

"That must be it," he said as he began to explain our results.

What he had never seen before were two people approaching every situation, all thirty-six scenarios, with exact and polar opposite approaches. Usually, he described, coming at things the way we did would be riddled with conflicts and disagreements. The bottom line: we loved each other and loved coming together. He ended our time with a warning. "Just make sure you keep on loving each other." *That* we fully intended to do.

We knew then and we know now equality cannot be earned. There are too many differences between us. Equality doesn't come from a side-by-side comparison. Equality is the gift and breath of love. We are equals in love. "God is love" the scriptures say, and equality with God can only be experienced as a result of being in love with God.

We command with official authority that life is good because God is good. "For the Lord is good; his love endures forever" (Jeremiah 33:11). "And God is working everything together for good, for those who love him and are the called according to his purpose" (Romans 8:28). This is our foundation. This is our primary confession.

We must believe that God is and that he rewards those who diligently seek him. God is for us. Jesus said, "Consider the lilies of the field ... how much more shall he clothe you, o ye of little faith" (Matthew 6:28–30). This is where our mind is kick-started—in the *how much more* of God in Jesus Christ! But, let's take the second step.

"but Caused Himself to Be Emptied ..."

All of us have baggage. We've all bought things we didn't need or never used. Time has been wasted. We've carried and continue to carry cares and anxieties that weigh us down and handicap our steps. To receive the gift of God, an exchange must be made. You must make it. You must cause yourself to be emptied. Your up-till-now way of doing things must be neutralized. The truth of God must take precedence over "life as you know it."

You can begin to draw new conclusions to old stories. How? Ask yourself these questions: Where in the narrative of my experience does a surprise need to be inserted? Where does a reversal of fortune or plot twist need to occur? Take a few minutes. Let the scenes of your life come under review. God has asked you to adapt that screenplay for a movie he is producing. God is calling for changes to the script. You are his hero or his heroine, and he is asking you to write out how the long-running conflicts will be resolved and overcome. The Holy Spirit will assist you.

Objectively set up each scene. What changes occur? How do you react differently this time? Spell out the ways God is with you. If you have time, go rent the movie *Stranger than Fiction*. How will the outcome of your life be different now that both the author of the story (God) and the character in the story (you) know each other?

This is what faith is all about—exchanging our tired screenplay for the epic adventure God has written for us in Jesus Christ. We are emptying ourselves of the lies and limitations under which our story has been diminished.

To move forward from here, we follow Jesus...

"And Took Upon Himself the Form of a Slave"

I don't work for myself anymore. I am bound to God, enslaved to Jesus. As the story of my life is written, Jesus is my editor-in-chief. I am not restricted to my old story, the opinion of others, or the spirit of this age. I am free to rewrite my story under the direct supervision of God.

Why do we, who value our freedom, take upon ourselves the form and attitude of a slave? It is the only way we can do anything God, our master, calls us to do. A slave cannot perform only the tasks he prefers. No, a slave does his work because the master has said it needs to be done.

To illustrate the power and freedom of this mindset, the late Dr. Edwin Louis Cole used to share this parable. If you were standing in your kitchen and you heard the voice of God say, "Sweep the floor," would you pick up the broom and believe God would give you the strength to wield it back and forth? The congregation would shake their heads up and down, "Yes."

Dr. Cole then would share, "Imagine you were driving down the highway and observed an accident. One of the victims is on the side of the road. A sheet is draped over them. You hear the same voice you heard in the kitchen say, 'Raise the dead.' Would you walk straight over to the body and command with authority for the dead to be raised? Why not? Wouldn't you believe God would give you the strength to wield his word that raises the dead?" Dr. Cole would add: "It's all the same to God—sweeping the floor, raising the dead. It's all a matter of obedience."

How much more will God accomplish through us when we take upon ourselves the form and mindset of a slave, emptying ourselves of the lies and prejudices we follow, opening ourselves to the freedom and delegated authority that is ours in Christ. All we do is follow. All we need do is obey.

We see our actions the same way God does. Authority obeyed equals ability displayed. This is why when the disciples needed to increase the strength of their faith they literally cried to Jesus, "Increase [Towards you] our faith!" (Luke 17: 5). We let nothing draw us away from standing with Jesus. Jesus bids us "Come" (Mark 14:29), and like Peter, we do not want a single wave to distract our focus away from Jesus. We simply respond to his voice.

As a slave, I attune myself to hear and obey only the master's voice. As a slave, I remember the power over my life and death is in the master's hands. It's good for me and for you that those hands are nail-scarred.

Yes, it is the voice of Jesus that turns me to service. It doesn't matter how urgent or pressing the needs or claims of others. The master takes precedent over everything else. We are above all God-pleasers. This is vital to remember as we are asked to be ...

"Made in the Likeness of Men ..."

This statement reveals the glorious humility of God in Jesus Christ. In the beginning God made man in his own likeness. Now Christ reverse engineers our restoration and salvation "caused to be made in the likeness of men."

"The Word became flesh and dwelt among us" (John 1:14, NKJV), and we observe that the strength and glory of Jesus is full of grace and truth. Jesus is full of compassion. He is full of endurance. He comes not to be served but to serve and give his life a ransom for many.

Our mind, our heart, responds to the same call and commission. We are made in the likeness of men. But, what does that mean? Galatians 4:4–5 says there are four defining elements that combine to make Jesus uniquely formed in the likeness of men.

First, Jesus had a mother. You and I do, too. We all came into the world the same way. Jesus came in flesh and blood. He was tempted, tested, and tried just like you and me; yet he remained without sin. Even though we all have sinned, Jesus knows what it is to be a child of mortal clay.

Second, Jesus came to be under the law. He had to receive his inalienable rights from God the Father just like you and me. No state or government gave him his status as an individual. No dictator or Caesar determined his life or his liberty. Jesus said himself, "It is written: 'Man does not live on bread alone, but on every word that comes from the mouth of God'" (Matthew 4:4). God makes the rules. Anyone who adds to God's word or subtracts from it will always make us less than human. Invariably, outside the law of God we become objects, consumers, or part of some anonymous group that others brandish about for their own will and profit.

We do not multiply laws to become an expression of the will of man through tradition or tyranny. Jesus said we do not need a multiplicity of rules and summed up the law and the prophets by commanding us to love God and to love our neighbor. Do this and live.

That's why the third element of being made in the likeness of men is how we can go to bat for one another. Jesus comes to redeem us, Paul says. He steps into the world's marketplace and purchases our freedom out from under the noses of those who seek to enslave us. He lifts us up even when we put ourselves down. Forgiveness leads Jesus' ministry and teaching.

The Bible teaches that we have all been slaves. We didn't have to make bricks without straw or be shackled together in lock step with others under a cruel overseer to be one. We hardened our hearts as slaves to suspicion and fear. We were dragged along by lust or addiction. We were moved only by our anger and ambition. We condemned ourselves to lies and weakness. Sin was our master.

To be made in the likeness of men is to know hope can change all that. We can have a dream, and the gracious love of God can make our dreams come true. To be made in the likeness of men is to approach every person knowing we share the need for mercy and deliverance. "Blessed be God, even the Father of our Lord Jesus Christ, the Father of mercies, and the God of all comfort; who comforted us in all our tribulation, that we may be able to comfort them which are in any trouble, by the comfort wherewith we ourselves are comforted of God" (2 Corinthians 1:3–4, kjv). We all share in trouble. The hope of being made in the likeness of men is that we all can also share in the comfort and power of God's deliverance through Jesus Christ.

To be made in the likeness of men is to stand responsible for one another because we stand accountable to God for how we live. Arm yourself with this same attitude.

The end of all things is near. Therefore be clear minded and self-controlled so that you can pray. Above all, love each other deeply, because love covers over a multitude of sins. Offer hospitality to one another without grumbling. Each one should use whatever gift he has received to serve others, faithfully administering God's grace in its various forms. If anyone speaks, he should do it as one speaking the very words of God. If anyone serves, he should do it with the strength God provides, so that in all things God may be praised through Jesus Christ. To him be the glory and the power for ever and ever. Amen.

1 Peter 4:7–11

Our relationship to others is based upon the mindset of Jesus who was "made in the likeness of men" (Philippians 2:7). We know this doesn't mean Jesus necessarily shares in our ethnicity or culture, our gender or sexuality, or our economic or political status. It means there is a common human experience that is greater than all of these. There is a larger and deeper reconciliation between us and God that is called for in Jesus Christ that breaks down all of those other barriers and differences.

This speaks to the fourth element of being made in the likeness of men. Jesus has come to fully restore our ability to operate and function as the sons of God. Greater than slaves who can obey their master, we can become the proud sons of the best "Daddy." "Because you are sons, God sent the Spirit of his Son into our hearts, the Spirit who calls out, 'Abba, Father.' So you are no longer a slave, but a son; and since you are a son, God has made you also an heir" (Galatians 4:6–7). Jesus learned how to operate this way, and we can too. Knowing this we can move to the next step.

"He Humbled Himself ... "

The humble man is one who can not only pursue and follow a more excellent way but also be followed. Jesus said, "Come unto me all you who labor and are heavy laden down and I will give you rest. Take my yoke upon you and learn of me (and you shall find rest for your souls) for I am meek and lowly in heart" (Matthew 11:28–29). Jesus said, "Come unto me because I am humble. I do not move men by force but faith. I do not change minds by compulsion but compassion." Jesus had guts, guts to act on behalf of others. He didn't use propaganda. His provocation was the plainness of his speech.

Persons like this cannot be bought or sold. They are fierce in their acts of justice and even fiercer in their love of mercy. Jesus is not a pacifist. He drives out evil, faces up to murderers, and rebukes those whose religion enslaves and kills. The crowds don't sway him by their wants or demands. He walks to the beat of his Father's touch.

Jesus is a humble man. He is a city set on a hill that cannot be hidden. He walks through the violent crowd. They cannot take him. He has power over his own life. No one can take his life.

He is reliable because the God/Father who he serves is reliable. We come to this humility when we can affirm we are who we are by the grace of God. We're honest. We'll admit we could be wrong. We will not shy away from righteous convictions. We will be unashamed of what is good. We will be unashamed of God.

The humble man is out to create a following but not for himself. Jesus cries out, "When a man believes in me, he does not believe in me only, but in the one who sent me. When he looks at me, he sees the one who sent me" (John 12:44). This is our cry. This is the cry of every humble heart.

Humility is not cowardice or fear. Humility is confidence in one greater than us. To humble ourselves is to express that confidence. I express it when I declare Jesus is Lord. I express it when I lay claim to every promise God gives. Our only fear should be having a lack of humility, for it is through the one who humbles himself that God can act and through which God's voice can be articulated most clearly.

How can this articulation of God's way be made clearer? How can our mindset be the same as Christ Jesus? It stands ready to take the final step.

"And Became Obedient Unto Death, Even the Death of the Cross ..."

Jesus said, "You must be born again" (John 3:7). If we are to experience all things becoming new, we must begin by voluntarily trusting ourselves to abide under the command of Jesus. This begins and ends in faith. Of all the scenarios we can follow in life, we decide to pursue the one where Jesus is Lord.

Jesus said, "If anyone wants to be my disciple, let him deny himself, take up his cross daily and follow me" (Luke 9:23). To share the mind of Christ we first share in the "want to." I want to be through with living life as a do-it-yourself project. I want to surrender as Jesus did on the cross and entrust my soul to a Faithful Creator (1 Peter 4:19). I turn to God right now and declare, "Into your hands I commit my spirit" (Luke 23:46).

I will be "swift to hear, slow to speak" (James 1:19, KJV). My life will have to change. To submit to following God's instruction means to listen attentively for God's voice. I commit myself daily to this pursuit. I will wake up every morning expecting God's direction. I will go to bed each night confident his words will fill my dreams. It's possible. The scriptures said, (The Shepherd) "He calls his own sheep by name and leads them out. When he has brought all his own, he goes on ahead of them, and his sheep follow him because they know his voice" (John 10:3–4).

Do you know the voice of Jesus? Have you decided to lay your life down and receive his? Are you committed to sharing the same mindset? If you said, "yes" then you're ready to proceed up the pathway of grace. You've made your beginning in repentance. It's now time to believe!

SMALL GROUP
DISCUSSION QUESTIONS

1. What words would you use to describe your love for God? How can this love help you to walk with God? How is love for God different from the love we have for others? Our spouse? Our child? Our friend?

2. Is there baggage you need to release, so you can be a servant of God? What is it? Are you able to put it down?

3. What does it mean to you that Jesus was willing to come to earth and live like us? Can this help you to respond to God's way of life instead of living in the ways of this world?

4. Does the word obedience scare you? Are you willing to set down your desires to listen for God's leading and then follow God?

Believe

Now faith is the substance of things hoped for, the evidence of things not seen.

> Hebrews 11:1

After John was put in prison, Jesus went into Galilee, proclaiming the good news of God. "The time has come," he said. "The kingdom of God is near. Repent and believe the good news!"

> Mark 1:14–15

The men who really believe in themselves are all in lunatic asylums.

> —G. K. Chesterton

SUBSTANTIATE YOUR FAITH

Beginning in repentance leads to believing. We believe and become a disciple, a part of God's team. God begins the work of molding us into the player who fits his way of doing things. Jesus is the ultimate player/coach, and he begins to teach us our place on the team and how to work everything together for good with him. One thing is required: faith.

Without faith all of a coach's instruction will fall on deaf ears. Without faith, we who have been aligned to God in repentance will continually kick ourselves out of alignment. Without faith, we who have chosen to accompany Jesus and be employed by him will show ourselves to be independent contractors who really want to be self-employed and still get employee benefits. Without faith, departing from evil will be a charade, a dramatic maneuver that only hides how lost and in bondage we still are.

What happens, then, when we do have faith? We can move forward into believing the Lord Jesus Christ and his word. Believing identifies who we are. Believing tells us who we are and who we belong to. Believing is an exchange we make between our biases, our way of looking at things, for God's way of looking at things. Faith gives us the opportunity to make this exchange.

We are able to make this exchange when we understand how faith comes. Jesus says, "My faith, the faith that leads to life, comes by hearing, and this hearing comes by the word of God." It is said that if we tell a lie often enough over and over again, everybody will believe it eventually. Why? Faith comes by hearing. We are to build ourselves up to be filled with the Word of God. We are to be rooted and grounded in faith so that we can comprehend all that God wants to do.

God is calling us to make sure we give attention and time to hear God's Word preached; to read God's Word and read good things; to watch good programs; to listen to the radio; to listen to music that leads to life and leads to faith. Faith in God—faith that leads to life—will not come by listening to trash-talk, vulgarities, profanities, vanities, or to fatalistic or hopeless scenarios. It just won't.

The Bible says, "Faith is the substance of things hoped for, the evidence of things not seen" (Hebrews 11:1, NKJV). We will never have greater faith by repeating what we've already experienced. Did you get that? For our faith to be substantial, we're going to have to introduce ourselves to new people, new godly people, to new places in the Scripture that we've never studied before. We're going to have to find people we can follow and see things from a different vantage point. We must trust and ask God for things that we have never experienced. One fault in the church is continually doing the same thing. Thus, our faith is never challenged and never increases. We have to continue to open ourselves to substantial things where up to now we haven't paid attention.

Hebrews 11 shows some of the things that faith will help you do and expect. It says, "By faith we understand that the universe was formed at God's command. So that what is seen was not made out of what was visible" (v. 30). By faith you can begin to explore the things that are not seen properly, the invisible things. God says that is really the first use of faith. That is, to understand that the things in the universe are made out of what is unseen. The key to our faith is seeing what is unseen. Moses was set apart from other people because the Bible says he looked on him who was invisible. He saw the invisible God.

In addition to seeing the unseen, faith can enable you to ask questions and find answers to the great mysteries of life. Ken Fisher, CEO of Fisher Investments and a *Forbes* magazine columnist, wrote the book *The Only Three Questions That Count: Investing by Knowing What Others Don't*. In this book Fisher lists three essential questions regarding investments that help you see things that others don't. His questions are these: What do I believe that is actually false? What can you fathom that others find unfathomable? What the heck is my brain doing to blindside me? Although Fisher's questions focus on successful methods for investing, they contain biblical applications. Thus, this chapter concludes with these three questions and explores how they can help us know whether we are substantiating our faith.

QUESTION 1:

What Do I Believe
That Is Actually False?

I have so many stories that I could share, lies that I have believed. The first one that I believed was when I was five-years-old. I grew up on a farm and my dad helped me plant a crop of sweet corn. I know you are thinking at five years old this plot of sweet corn is about two feet by three feet. No, it was much larger, thirty yards by fifteen yards. When the crop grew, it was the prettiest corn you ever saw. It was only about a week away from harvesting. All the tassels had come out, and it was just beautiful.

During this time, my family decided to go on a three-day vacation. Three days was fine. My corn wouldn't be ready for probably another week. I would have plenty of time to come back, harvest, and eat all that good corn. When we returned from vacation, we discovered the cows ate all of my corn down to the ground. All the cows had gotten out of the pasture and gorged themselves on my sweet corn.

I was devastated. Do you know what I decided? I decided I could never become a farmer. I could never become a farmer even though I had demonstrated I already could be one by how great the crop was and how beautifully it had grown and how ready for harvest it was. Do you know what? I am not a farmer. Not to say I couldn't go back and be one, but you have to ask yourself what do you believe that is actually false. It was actually false that I could never be a farmer.

I have had folks tell me that I could not sing. I am thankful that when I was young I wanted to sing so bad I kept on trying. Even when they told me my voice wasn't so good, I thought, *Okay, other voices are good. I will sing like other people.*

I began to sing and use the voice of other people. I could sound like Neil Diamond or Johnny Mathis. Rich Little, the impressionist, was very popular then. I thought if he could do regular voices I could sing like other people. I could sing like Jim Croce or James Taylor. I would get an opportunity every once in a while to sing because people would want to hear my impersonations, even though I had been told that I could not sing.

Last, the men in my family had a history of never finishing what we started. We never did what we set out to do. My grandfather wanted to be a doctor, but due to circumstances, he never became one. He became a good principal and a great worker for the soil conservation service. He helped a lot of people, but never became the doctor he had in his mind to become. My grandfather was offered property when he bought our farm. We grew up on a 115-acre farm. He had money enough to buy about three thousand acres, but he couldn't see how he would manage all of that. He told himself, *There is not a way for me to ever learn how to work that much land,* which wasn't true. He could have. He could have learned how to manage that land, and what a difference that would have made in our family. He believed the lie he told himself.

My dad had the opportunity to work in a store, daily interacting with people, which would have been perfect for him. He never pursued it because others, particularly his daddy (my grandfather) told him that he just didn't see how he would ever make it. He gave his consent to the discouragement rather than the encouragement.

What do you believe that is actually false? That is the first question faith will ask itself. It is a good question. We are creatures of faith. We were created to live by faith. How do I know this? Because our eyes don't tell our brain what we see, our brain tells our eyes what we see. We interpret by our faith experience what we see in the world. So, ask yourself the first question in substantiating your faith: "What do I believe that is actually false?"

QUESTION 2:

What Can You Fathom
That Others Find Unfathomable?

What can you fathom that others find unfathomable? In other words, what things will you keep on asking God and believing God for until you have them? Jesus says, "Ask, believing that you shall receive them and you shall have them" (Matthew 21:22). Do you believe until you figure you are not going to get what you're praying for and then quit believing? Are there areas of your life where you have already shut down on exploring because you have said to yourself, "I will never get that. I will never understand that." If the answer is yes, think about Fisher's question once more: "What can you fathom that others find unfathomable?" If you put your faith in Jesus Christ, your life was changed and you were converted. That is already something that you fathomed that others find unfathomable. Now, think about other areas of your life where you need to open up yourself and allow faith to operate. In addition, it is so important to read the lives and testimonies of others so you can see God work and do miracles. Your faith can be substantiated, strengthened, refined, focused, and stronger than it was before.

The church in the United States needs to open itself to the revival that is taking place in other parts of the world. We don't want to be closed to it. We don't want to make light of it. I had an older lady in one of the churches I once served. She was probably around eighty years old, and I shared the rate of growth that was occurring in the African church, particularly the United Methodist church in Mozambique. I told her how quickly it was expanding and how marvelously it was growing. She replied from a mindset of experiencing a church that hadn't grown and hadn't changed in forty years. She said, "Well, they must be mighty immature people." She said, "They must be awfully immature to grow that fast." She could not fathom in her experience how a church would grow and people would be open to the good news of Jesus and how their whole life could be changed.

We have to find ways to fathom what others find unfathomable. All the older lady had to do was investigate and discover what was already occurring beyond her limited experience. Then she had to ask God for the same kind of results in her own life. She could even ask that her vision of life be expanded. Maybe her church wouldn't grow as fast. Maybe the receptivity of others wouldn't be the same, but that is all right. She could still understand and fathom what was unfathomable. That is how we begin to substantiate our faith. To ask these questions: What do you actually believe that is actually false? What can you fathom that others find unfathomable?

I remember one time when my wife Karen and I had a pressing need. We hadn't been married long and didn't have much income, if any. We had a medical emergency, received treatment, and then they sent us a bill. Fancy that. We didn't have any money to pay the bill. I know the custom of doctors is that they will send us another bill if we don't respond to the first. When they sent the second bill, we may have paid very little on it. When they sent the next bill, they sent a letter that said they would come to see us and personally collect on the bill. I didn't know what to do. It was unfathomable how we would pay that bill. We wanted our faith to be substantiated. I asked God, "What can I do?" Karen and I both prayed and sought God about how to pay this bill. We were working as hard as we could at the time, but we just weren't getting paid very much.

We got the bill on Friday, so Saturday came and we prayed and sought God. I thought the only thing to do was go to church on Sunday and look for the person who God was going to lead our way to pay our bill. I didn't know what else to do.

We were attending a rather large church at the time, and I went to all three services that morning. I was waiting to meet the person who would be led by God to come and help us, and they never showed up. I kept on waiting for them to come.

I went on back home, and again I prayed, "God, please. This bill needs to be paid, and we don't know how it is going to be paid." We wouldn't have put it in these terms, but we wanted to fathom what was unfathomable. At the very least, we wanted God to fathom what was unfathomable and then let us in on it.

The very next day inside our mailbox was a letter from my sister. We received the bill on Friday. The letter from my sister was postmarked on Thursday, so it was sent even before we got the bill. Inside was a little note that said, "Dear Norman and Karen. We were praying for you all and felt like God wanted us to send you this. Kind of weird. Love, Janet."

Inside was a check for one hundred fifty-three dollars and fifty-one cents. Do you want to guess how much our bill was? One hundred fifty-three dollars and fifty-one cents. You need to find a way in your heart to fathom what is unfathomable or at least ask God to fathom it for you and then let you in on it. That is the way we substantiate our faith.

QUESTION 3:
What the Heck Is My Brain Doing to Blindside Me?

What the heck is my brain doing to blindside me? Your brain is the battlefield of your soul. God commands its allegiance through repentance and obeying the truth. Our sin nature and our enemy seek to control our brains through temptation and deceit. When it comes to faith, the enemy tries to distort what we can expect from God. He tries to diminish it. He tries to nullify it and cancel it out.

Fisher tells us there are two basic reasons why our brain blindsides us. One is because it is trying to accumulate pride for itself. It is trying to look good, trying to get accolades and praise instead of giving it to God. It is just the way it works. You ought to be aware of it. Jeremiah 17:9 says, "our heart (our brain) is desperately wicked." In other words, it is distorted and deceitful above all things. You might say "I am not like that, I see things plainly." No, you don't, because your brain interprets for you and then tells you what you see.

This story illustrates the point. Karen and I moved back into my family's home place in the country. Across the road from our house was a little rental house where the state trooper lived. Of course, he had his gray state trooper car. I can remember several times when I was ready to pull out of our driveway. I looked both ways to see if anything was coming, and my brain told my eyes nothing was coming. In reality, a car was coming. But my brain saw the oncoming gray vehicle and parked it in the driveway across the street—the categorical spot where all gray cars exist. When I pulled out of our driveway, the horn was blaring of the actual gray car that was coming up the highway right past my driveway. That happened more than once.

You see we need to ask ourselves, *What the heck is my brain doing to blindside me?* Your brain knows what it thinks it knows, but not necessarily, because your brain will try to accumulate pride. There is a way that seems right to man, but the end is the way of death. Your brain would never try to steer you wrong, but its ideal of right may be messed up. So we will expect to have to ask, "What the heck is my brain doing to blindside me?" so that our faith can be substantiated.

Fisher says not only does our brain try to accumulate pride, but it also tries to avoid regret. I don't know any of us who enjoy or relish the opportunity of humbling ourselves before other people and saying we were wrong. I don't know where the great apologizers are. I haven't met many of them.

Not only does faith come by hearing and hearing by the Word of God, faith is the substance of things hoped for, the evidence of things not seen. The Bible says that faith works by love. That is why we want to substantiate our faith so that we always know it is working by love. It works by the love of God. It works because God is with us. God is alive in us. God is speaking to us. God is directing us. God is leading us. We are living according to his word, his word of love.

I am thankful for the questions Fisher asks in his book. I am thankful that God calls us to exchange our way, our blindness, and our biased way of looking at things, for his way of looking at things.

If you are going to move forward and get up to speed with God, then you're going to have to substantiate your faith. You're going to have to allow faith to come to you by hearing and hearing by the Word of God.

You're going to have to begin to fathom that which is unfathomable, to see those unseen things that others can't see. God is asking you by faith to see it. Smith Wigglesworth, a great evangelist of the nineteenth century, said, "One minute of faith is worth a lifetime of all the other of God's gifts." He is right. If you have just a moment of faith, your whole life can be changed. Let God come to you by faith. Let God substantiate your faith.

Faith is by necessity personal. If we believe in principles or universals only, we miss the most essential aspect of faith: Faith is for relationships. Galatians 5:6 tells us, "the only thing that counts is faith expressing itself by love." I believe in gravity. I believe in methods of exchange using various forms of currency. But The Beatles were right. Methods of exchange using various forms of currency or "money," can't buy me love. Gravity works. It just exists as a fact of life. Faith works by love. When the Apostle Paul speaks of access into this grace in which we stand in Romans chapter 5, he's not talking about some universal, fuzzy, spiritual hall pass that's available upon request. He's talking about the personal favor and direction of Jesus.

It is only in faith that the exchange of our ways for God's can be made. Believing carries us into the life of God. It draws us outside of ourselves and brings us to a place of interconnection. The Apostle Paul says, "Being justified by faith, we have peace with God through our Lord Jesus Christ" (Romans 5:1, KJV). This peace is the byproduct of substantial faith. Our connection to God arises out of our confidence in him. Proverbs 3:4–6 advises us to "trust in the Lord with all your heart, and lean not unto your own understanding [but] in all your ways acknowledge Him, and He shall direct your paths" (NKJV). Those paths will follow one of two ways: the pathway of sin or the pathway of grace. Sin follows the way of division and separation from God. Grace follows the way of peace.

In this chapter I have stressed the importance of substantiating your faith, knowing what others don't. The first thing you must know is the way of peace. You are created to know deep and thorough connectivity to God. This comes from Jesus Christ "for he is our peace" (Ephesians 2:14). This is not your original condition because each of us has sinned and fallen short of the glory of God (Romans 3:23). I am asking you to exchange your original condition in sin for a new and substantial condition of faith. Just as we have always known we were sinners, I am asking you to now know with equal or greater conviction we are "justified freely by his grace through the redemption that came by Christ Jesus" (Romans 3:24). This is how God sees us; how he foreknows us—as the Redeemed, the Righteous, and ones who have a substantial faith in Jesus Christ.

SMALL GROUP DISCUSSION QUESTIONS

1. Are you willing to challenge your faith in order to grow in your relationship with God?

2. What have you attempted over and over in your faith journey that results in remaining in the same place?

3. Discuss with the group your answers to Ken Fisher's three questions.

4. If we live a life of faith, we will have peace also. Share with others about the areas of your life where you would like to have peace.

FOLLOWING GOD'S LEAD INTO FAITH

I was raised in a great environment for believing God. My parents were devout Christians. They loved God, and they loved each other. They were not perfect, but I have no horror stories to tell. In fact, I have wonderful stories from a childhood spent on the three farms owned by my grandfather and his two brothers. It was a multigenerational, extended family motion picture of God working everything together for our good.

Though both of my parents were happy to be finished with their formal education graduating from high school, they inspired in each of their four children an insatiable, intellectual curiosity. Before there was such a thing as kindergarten or preschool, we were taught to read and write. The highlight of that time for me was learning to spell *elephant* before I learned to spell my own name. We were taught to tell time and count by the time we were four. My love for the way of words was birthed when learning to read by an old Holman King James Bible. It was the first present I ever received.

I was taught God was at work in the midst of our lives. I believed I could talk to animals, and I did. I called up birds to join me on the back steps. I serenaded the cows, commanding their attention and movement, and even had my own version of Arnold the pig like Mr. Ziffel on Green Acres.

I learned the signs of sky and land for the weather in our area. If we needed rain, we asked for it and expected the signs to follow. We were not superstitious. Every prayer was grounded in a scriptural promise. We discovered there were good and well-founded reasons for following God.

Following God's ways was simply the most reliable, faithful way to go. We demonstrated that in ninth grade Earth Science class when we studied weather. Our forecasts for the six weeks were ninety-six percent accurate while the National Weather Service's forecasts were eighty-six percent accurate for the same period.

Both then and looking back now, believing in God through his Son, Jesus Christ, was and is the best thing I can do. Your faith will have to find its own shape as mine has. You will need to substantiate your faith and allow it to become the rock solid foundation upon which you build your life. But, its shape should be molded by the pattern and path God paves for us in his Word.

In chapter 3 we examined Philippians 2, which revealed how we could develop the mind of Christ—shaping our beginning in repentance to follow Jesus. To further shape and substantiate our believing we turn to Psalm 23. As we explore Psalm 23 in this chapter, we will find the Lord our Shepherd ready to lead us into a deep and abiding relationship of trust.

"The Lord Is Our Shepherd; I Shall Not Want."

The Lord loves us. He oversees our life out of kindness. He leads by example, going before us, taking the initiative to share his life with us.

God is not out to get us or condemn us. However, for most of us that could be easily done. God could have dealt harshly with me as a child for stealing the church money. My grandfather was church treasurer. I don't remember what prompted me to take the money in the first place, but take it I did. I remember hiding behind the pump house counting the ways I could benefit from this loot. That's when the voice of my conscience (call it your personal antenna for the voice of God) said, "Put the money back. It's not yours. Put it back before you get caught. You'll be ruined if you don't." I put the money back. I don't know if my grandfather knew I had taken it out of his desk drawer or not, but I knew God had seen. No posse came. No jailor showed up. Nothing came. God was not out to get me. God was leading me to a place of sufficiency and confidence.

When I climbed up the tree on the west side of the house at age three, I entered a new world. I could see for a hundred miles. I also noticed after I got to the top that I could see how far it was to the ground. I called for Mama, who was hanging clothes on the line, to come and save me. A breeze had picked up, and I was sure the swaying treetop was the place from which I would take my final flight. I pleaded with Mama to get me down. "You got up there. Get yourself down," she replied. Well, I write today because somehow I got down.

The same feeling returned when my daddy asked me as a teenager to work on the top poles of the tobacco barn. I had worked on the bottom where the poles are a foot thick, sturdy and immovable. Up on top they were flimsy and bounced when you shifted your weight. I wasn't sure I could work there without falling. Daddy was sure I could.

When Psalm 23 says, "I shall not want," it means I shall not *be* in want. I shall not abide, stay, take up residence, or allow myself to be identified with what I lack. No, I shall be identified by what I love and have in Jesus Christ. It is interesting to note a subtle difference between the crowds that followed Jesus and the disciples who followed Jesus. The crowds were primarily identified by where they came from. The disciples were identified primarily by where they were going.

How are you identified? How do you introduce yourself? By your fears or your faith? By your difficulties or your possibilities? By your dilemmas or your dreams?

How are you gauging or judging your actions? By how high you can climb or how far you can fall? By the shadows that follow you or the Shepherd who leads you?

"He Makes Me to Lie down in Green Pastures. He Leads Me Beside the Still Waters."

The goal of faith is to bring you to a place of safety. It's not the kind of safety that Linus of Peanuts® fame experienced with his blanket. It's not the kind of safety found behind locked doors or in padded rooms. It is not derived from warning labels or laws. It is the kind of safety I felt when I rode a motorcycle as a young man. Some said I was wild, even crazy, but they were wrong. What I was was well practiced.

My brother and I used to race in the pasture. In order for me to win I would have to go twice as fast. 2 to 1 odds gave each of us each an equal opportunity at victory.

I also occasionally jumped with the motorcycle on a hill in the pasture. Using the contour of the land, you could glide 120 feet through the air before you touched down. Was I crazy? No, I was being faithful to my limits. To accomplish this jump you could only go twenty-seven miles per hour. If you went any faster, you overran the dip at the top of the hill and simply drove down the hill.

You see, faith is finding our limits and then asking God to take us beyond them. Just as repentance is a stretch from where we have been to where God wants us to be, so faith is a stretch, a movement from where we are to where God is going.

Faith in God through our Lord Jesus affirms that God is leading us toward being nourished and refreshed. Sometimes that nourishment seems hard to swallow as we are asked to give thanks and receive everything that is on our plate. I remember my oldest son's experience when he was at boot camp. He was at breakfast, and his drill sergeant suggested he not eat any doughnuts. Was the drill sergeant trying to be restrictive? I suppose you could say, "Yes," but I like to think he was trying to keep my son safe from getting sick during the training that followed breakfast.

My parents led me to green pastures and to still waters. Most often that leadership was positive, attesting to their faith in me, telling me I could do anything and anything I chose to do I would do well. I never had a curfew or other kinds of restrictions. What I did have were my grandmother's parting words to me before I left home for a date: "Be careful, and be a gentleman."

Less often that leadership was expressed in some prohibition. I can still remember the time my daddy told me to stop seeing one particular girl. I had suddenly started seeing a lot of this girl, riding over to her house only a few miles away from ours. It was just starting to get interesting. However, because this kind of admonition was so rare coming from Daddy, I immediately stopped seeing her. Believing clarifies not through sight but through trust. Sight verification comes later. A year or so later, this particular girl had the baby of the next guy that suddenly started dating her.

"He Restores My Soul."

Faith is going to encourage us to exchange bad habits for good. Faith is going to ask us and lead us to exchange our thinking for the thoughts of God. Our actions will be commanded to change.

Faith working by love frames the process of our soul's restoration—the restoration of our will, our mind, and our emotions. The Lord our Shepherd has faith in us. This faith is active and restorative. This faith and this work are directed toward our soul because of the Shepherd's great love.

Pay attention to the order of the Lord's restorative work. It begins with our will. Is it proving its alignment to Jesus? Are we obedient to the voice of God—instantly, without rationalization or calculation? The Bible says faith comes or increases in value by hearing and hearing by the Word of God. This hearing carries an implied obedience. So the power of faith, the power of believing, increases in value as obedience is willfully offered to God's leadership.

This reminds me of a time when my obedience was not willfully offered. It was summertime on the farm. We had been swimming in our pond, but the cows were starting to have an undue influence on the quality of the water. My sister Janet didn't want to swim in the pond anymore. Since she didn't want to, Mama wouldn't take just Dennis and me. What were boys to do? We asked Daddy for help, and he agreed to build us a whole new place to swim.

Daddy, Uncle Jack, and my grandfather built a dam on the creek on the backside of our farm. It formed a great swimming pool, and our family was having a wonderful time enjoying our inaugural swim. In the midst of this, I was climbing in and out of the swimming pool, walking across the dam, and diving back in. On one of these trips I was standing on the dam when I heard my daddy cry out to me, "Jump in!" I knew he was calling me. I knew exactly what he meant, but instead of obeying, I looked around to see what the reason could be for him wanting me to jump in. By the time I found out, the yellow jackets had already stung me six times.

We have been given an invitation by Jesus. Have faith in God. Taste and see that the Lord is good. Jump into a relationship of obedient faith. Willfully obey, and multiply your confidence because the restorative work of the soul begins in our will.

We renew our mind as we become more familiar with the content and intent of God's word. Paul told his son in the faith, Timothy, to devote himself to reading, preaching, and teaching. Learn to rely on what's reliable.

When John Wesley was uncertain of his relationship with God, a Moravian friend told him to preach faith until he had it and after that preach faith. Use your mouth to confess the faith. Let your mouth serve as a feedback loop to your brain.

Write down and repeat the promises of God. There is nothing more mind refreshing than reading or confessing something out of the scripture and seeing it replicated later. It brings joy to your soul. It was neat to read about this happening in my youngest son's life recently. Robert had just started basic training and all of his first letters talked about how hungry he was. Mealtime is very compressed, but one Sunday things were different. Robert had read from chapter twelve of Luke's Gospel, where Jesus says, "Don't worry about what you shall eat or drink. Your Father knows you have need of these things."

Robert said he laughed later at the thought of reading these verses that day. He and his battle buddy had early guard duty. After that, the drill sergeant led them to the mess hall. As they began to go down the chow line, Robert commented on how good the food was and how he wished he could eat more. The lady serving them overheard his comments, and instead of the usual rations, she piled their plates up with food. The sergeant even left the mess hall giving them extra time to enjoy this abundant provision.

Jesus said we will live by every word that proceeds from the mouth of God. Make sure your mind wraps itself around that. It'll make you laugh out loud. It'll make you feel as Jim Carrey says in Bruce Almighty—"Gooood!"

The last point of restoration affects our feelings, our emotions. Feelings don't come first. Faith works by love, and in the Bible love is not about what you feel but what you do. So, restoration of our souls follows this equation: Action + Adjustments = Attitude. Feelings follow.

Now it's wonderful if feelings are aligned at the beginning with our actions. But, we would prove very immature people if we only acted when we have good feelings. Acting in good faith implies we will do what is right regardless of how we feel. Jesus operates out of this same equation: Action + Adjustments = Attitude. In the Gospel of Matthew, at the end of chapter eleven, Jesus offers this invitation to restoration: "Come unto me all that labor and are heavy laden down and I will give you rest. Take my yoke upon you and learn from me; for I am lowly in heart, and you shall find rest for your souls" (Matthew 11:28–29). Action (Come) + Adjustments (Take/Learn) = Attitude (Rest)

Mike Litman encourages us when he says, "You don't have to get it right; you just have to get it going." In any undertaking, take action, get feedback, make adjustments, and hone your product or service to meet your target audience. If you wait for perfect conditions nothing will ever get done. Rick Bonfim adds the worst possible spiritual situation is being parked on P: paralyzed, unwilling, unable to move. The presence of God in our lives implies movement and action.

"He Leads Me in Paths of Righteousness
for His Name's Sake. Yes, Though I Walk Through
the Valley of the Shadow of Death, I Will Fear
No Evil. Your Rod and Staff They Comfort Me."

John Wesley once stated, "The best thing of all is God is with us." I agree with him. It is the source of our confidence. We do not need to be afraid when trying something for the first time or terrified by the consequences of doing something wrong. Jesus, our Emmanuel, will be himself, faithful and true. Discipline and direction are the twin gifts he is constantly ready to give. But, often we misread what God is doing. The fact of faith that God is with us, leading us down a very personal path of righteousness, is always worked out in the valleys of our lives. As I've said before, I believe I had one of the world's greatest dads. But there were moments when my faith in him was put to the test.

One of those moments came when I was twelve. That was the year I would win the Punt, Pass, & Kick competition. I tried to forget what happened the year before. I was leading the competition by a large margin after the punt and the pass. I lined up for the kick when the official said I had to kick with tennis shoes. I only had dress shoes.

The official said I could kick barefooted, but I knew all I would do was hurt my toes. Jon Stenereud of the Kansas City Chiefs was the only person I had ever seen kick soccer style. I didn't know how to do that. I pleaded with the official to let Mama or Daddy go home and get my tennis shoes. Forty minutes is all it would take.

No, it was my turn to kick, and I would be disqualified if I didn't take my turn. All I could do was try. My interpretation—all I could do was fail.

Each phase of the competition is measured by distance minus accuracy. I had almost nothing taken away for my punt or my pass. My kick, punched off the tee by my big toe, spiraled up and away from the distance line giving me a negative yard and spiraled me down from first place to third.

I knew the next year would be different. That year when we left for our vacation, I put my tennis shoes in the car. Daddy promised he would get me back in time for the competition. I had practiced. I was ready but Daddy forgot his promise—forgot me.

I stayed quiet as we drove by the football field, my tennis shoes already on. I stared silently as the other boys warmed up, their dads standing beside them. Everybody else in the car was excited we were finally almost home. I didn't say anything. When we got home I was asked why I looked so sad. I told them we missed the competition. Why hadn't I said something? I didn't think I had to. Daddy had promised.

Daddy was my rock. He rarely disappointed. Maybe that's why, when it did happen, it was such a hard thing to deal with. The truth is there's only one other moment I can share. It happened in high school. Dennis and I had been invited to sing and tour in Europe. Daddy said he could only afford to send one of us on this trip. I could decide who got to go. Dennis went to Europe. A year later we got invited to the Fred Waring Music Camp in Pennsylvania. Again Daddy came to me and asked me to decide who got to go. Dennis went to music camp. I could have made the decision to go myself but not really. Daddy did a lot of things for me, but I wish choosing to send me instead of choosing to let me decide had been one of them. I didn't realize the double opportunity he was giving me. He gave me the chance to go on these trips and the opportunity to make it my own choice. The shadows of the valley marred that perspective.

Years later, Karen and I moved to Nashville. I went to be a songwriter. I didn't realize that meant I went to meet the best editors who would make me a better songwriter. My faith was so small my first draft was the best I could do. Others had greater faith. I didn't. I quit, went to work somewhere else, and didn't write another song for almost six years.

Don't miss the greatest blessing of faith and confuse it for something bad. "I will fear no evil" really means that. I will not fear what seems hard, mean, or critical as a sign God is not with me or a sign that I'm wrong and need to quit. The greatest blessing of faith confesses what is true. I could've done this by saying, "Dad, I know everybody wants to get home, but you promised I could Punt, Pass, & Kick first. I just wanted to remind you."

I could've said, "Dad, I appreciate you letting me make the decision on this trip. Dennis is a great worker, and he will help you while I go this time."

I could've said, "Michael (the music executive), I thank you for seeing so much potential in my writing. I want to do whatever it takes to become the best writer this town has ever known." I could've said that, but I did not. I forgot God was at work in my life.

Faith remembers God's rod and staff are at work. Then, when faith remembers, faith begins to recognize the ways comfort and strength is being supplied. Faith that forgets is an immature faith. It is easily defeated, quickly made cynical, and fails because of fear.

Yes, my faith has been extremely immature at times. The good news is God's word is true. "Yes, though I walk through the valley of the shadow of death"—the death of my hopes, the death of my dreams, and the death of my confidence—"You are with me. Your rod and your staff they comfort me."

I will no longer fear the valley of shadows. Faith, my faith, will remember God's first call to accompany him as he works everything together for my good! My faith will remember.

"You Prepare a Table Before Me in the Presence of My Enemies."

Yes, we can all be immature or shortsighted in our faith of God's affirming presence and work. Our fears limit the work of God. Some of us have even lost our faith, but this is not our calling or destiny. God wants our faith to be strong and shared. This sharing is specifically assisted by God when it is done with those who have the "least" of faith.

I can remember when some of Keith's friends came over to our home for the first time. We sat down at the dining room table for supper together, and they didn't know what to do. They had never sat down as a family to eat a meal. They didn't know to give thanks for the food before the meal. They were not familiar with passing the food around the table or choosing portions so everyone could have plenty. They didn't know to voice their appreciation for the meal after they finished. We had to show them and model for them how it was done. We enjoyed sharing those meals together and eventually even taught them how to set the table themselves.

The psalmist declares God does the same thing with us. The Lord our Shepherd sets a table for us. He sets in order the table of contents for our life's story. He arranges our very existence in time and space. Did you know I was supposed to be stillborn? Yep, Mama had had a miscarriage the year before. They expected something similar to happen to me after she went for the fifth-month doctor's visit. As she left the office that morning, her water broke.

They went back in, but the doctor said there was nothing he could do at that point. He discreetly told Daddy not to let Mama get her hopes up. Two months later, two months premature, I was born—a dry baby. One big wrinkle was how they described me.

My great aunt told me as a child that I had started small and probably would never amount to anything big. We had a history assignment in the sixth grade and were told to chronicle on a time-line the significant historical dates in Virginia history. The year 1959 I listed two historical events: the construction of the Chesapeake Bay Bridge Tunnel and my birth. My teacher, Mr. Jackson, dropped my score a letter grade with the comment that my birth had as yet no historical significance. I told him he was being unfairly premature.

I know my steps have been graciously ordered by the Lord. How else would you explain the little boy who went to see bologna sliced on a machine as a child for entertainment, eating at a churrascaria in Rio de Janeiro? How would you explain the story of a boy who was not good enough to sing in a sixth grade rock band but performed at Disney World and heard Roy Acuff say, "That boy sure can sing," as he walked off the stage of the Grand Old Opry? How would you explain the story of a young man who was told he could never be a good pastor or been asked if he had been diagnosed with ADHD preaching the world's longest sermon or writing and finishing this book for you to read?

How would I explain it? I would say the Lord was preparing a table before me in the presence of my enemies. The Lord prepared the table and set a place for Rick Bonfim, a United Methodist evangelist who encouraged me to go to Brazil. The Lord prepared a table and set a place for Rich Little, the impressionist, so I could be inspired to sing like other people if my voice wasn't so good at the start. The Lord prepared a table and set a place for Glenn Dietzel and Ronda DelBoccia at AwakentheAuthorWithin.com and gave me encouragement to write this book.

The Lord is preparing a table for you, too. Don't be alarmed at who shows up for dinner. Just as your faith receives its most pointed blessing in the valley, it will find its most flavorful expression in front of your enemies. The enemies the Scripture speaks of here are those people brought into our lives who seek to cramp our trust in God. They are our adversaries because they want to narrow and limit the effect faith has on us. The table God has prepared for you is especially set in front of them.

They don't know how to give thanks for their own table. They probably have never sat down and felt like they belonged or were welcome at a meal. They are not familiar with passing the food around the table or choosing portions so everybody can have plenty. They might have been taught it's impossible for everybody to have plenty. So they are apprehensive to voice their appreciation for the meal after they finished. Who will guarantee in this age of scarcity where the next meal will come from?

This is our job. This is our calling. We will guarantee that wherever we abide, grace will abide there as well. That grace will prove sufficient since it arises from the riches of God's glorious provision. We will in our generosity swamp their paucity. When their fears make it hard for us to swallow our daily bread, we will clear our throats and remind them they are always welcome at our table. The good food will never run out. We have a very powerful and well stocked supplier: the Lord our Shepherd.

"He Anoints My Head with Oil. My Cup Runs over. Surely Goodness and Mercy Shall Follow Me All the Days of My Life and I Will Dwell in the House of the Lord Forever."

God is invested in our life. "For God so loved the world that he gave his only begotten Son that whosoever believes in him shall not perish but have everlasting life" (John 3:16). The Lord our Shepherd has called us to a life of faith, and he is faithful to lead, restore, comfort, and cover us until that faith is complete.

The time when my daddy died was the same season when God coordinated the events of my life and enabled me to go to Brazil. Others had tried to describe this great country to me. It was a trip back home for me. The little shacks on the hill, dirt paths, and old appliances reminded me of Grandma's. She never had indoor plumbing. Water was brought up from the spring. She had a two-seater outhouse in the backyard. The most delicious food was made from an old wood stove. God anointed my head with oil. My cup ran over at every turn with the memories and childlike confidence.

The anointing oil was smeared on the sheep in the fall to protect them and preserve them as winter was approaching. In the same way, God smears his grace on thick, filling every nook and cranny of our lives. Our faith is secured by God himself, sealed with a guarantee—the indwelling Holy Spirit. It is the Holy Spirit who will reveal the way of Jesus to us, glorifying the Father through the tracks we leave on our journey.

God's goodness and mercy shall follow us and overtake us. Our faith will be built up for the valleys we have to walk through and for the table we will set. Others will be walking through those same valleys. Others will be hungry and thirsty for what the Lord has poured out to you and me. We must now get ready to move further up the pathway of grace . We get ready to "build up your most holy faith praying in the Holy Spirit" (Jude 1:20, KJV).

SMALL GROUP
DISCUSSION QUESTIONS

1. How do you know God as a shepherd who is leading you on a growing spiritual journey?

2. Do you know the place of green pastures and still waters? What actions might help you to know these places and then be restored?

3. When have you walked through a dark valley? Did you look for God's guidance and direction during that time? Are you better able to do it now when a dark time comes to your life?

4. As you live your faith life in front of others who think it is not possible to grow in grace on the path God is calling you, where can you see your cup overflowing and blessings multiplying?

Build Up Your Most Holy Faith

But you, dear friends, build yourselves up in your most holy faith and pray in the Holy Spirit. Keep yourselves in God's love as you wait for the mercy of our Lord Jesus Christ to bring you to eternal life.

Jude 20:2

Nothing will be impossible for you.

Matthew 17:20

Have I not commanded you? Be strong and courageous. Do not be terrified; do not be discouraged, for the Lord your God will be with you wherever you go.

Joshua 1:9

BUILD UP YOUR FAITH

George Michael sang, "You gotta have faith." But that faith must be substantiated by the Word of God and by the spirit of the Good Shepherd. It must be built into a faith that works by love. Learning how to pray in the power of the Holy Spirit is the most direct means to that goal.

The first prayer I ever learned was a prayer of committal. "Now I lay me down to sleep, I pray the Lord my soul to keep. If I should die before I wake, I pray the Lord my soul to take." Next, I learned a prayer of praise and thanks. Even though it didn't follow the traditional model, it still worked. "God is good. God is great. Let us thank him for our food. Amen." My parents had their own grace at the table—Mama at breakfast and dinner, Daddy at supper. It was said so fluid that it took me a while to get it. "Lord, make us thankful for these and for all our many blessings. Pardon our sins, we beg for Christ's sake. Amen."

You may have had different prayers that marked your childhood. For many years I prayed "God bless" prayers. Every request began with God bless, and then I would fill in the blank starting with my immediate family, then uncles, aunts, and cousins, then outward to the rest of the world. My daughter does a variation of that. Hers is a "God help" prayer most of the time.

All of this works together for good toward each of us building a loving and lasting relationship with God. Recently, God showed me a way I could pray that was true to the pathway of prayer Jesus teaches in the Lord's Prayer and true to me. I call it the Seven S's. There are seven S's to reflect my love of alliteration and seven S's to cultivate my faith and my relationship with God. They are below:

1. Stand

2. Sing

3. Scripture

4. Supplication

5. Stations

6. Silence

7. Sending Steps

I can pray through them in two minutes or two hours. This pattern for prayer reflects how my relationship with God has grown. I asked God to give me a *way* of praying, and God did.

This is how I follow each step. I begin by taking my stand with God in repentance. Stand comes from Ephesians 5. My life stands apart unto God as I give reverence to him and hallow his name. I stand against the schemes of the evil one. I stand alert to the movement called forth by the work of the Holy Spirit in me.

Next, I sing. Singing is how I most clearly and articulately declare what I believe. I once held the record for the world's longest sermon. Ask anybody, and the person will tell you I talk too much. But, if I had to be limited to only one expression of my faith, it would be in what I sing. In singing, whether it is a hymn or a spur of the moment original, I share my desire for God's kingdom to come and God's will to be done.

Third, scripture is what feeds the heart of my prayer. It echoes the voice of God. Rick Bonfim says fifty percent of all revelation is in knowing what the scripture says. When I ask God to give me my daily bread, I am asking God to prescribe for me what is fitting for the day. How beautiful is that? Proverbs 25:11 says, "A word fitly spoken is like apples of gold in pictures of silver" (KJV). I marvel at God's faithful communication of his grace day in and day out through his Word.

Let me give you one example. I lead a worship service at our local hospital for those who need long-term care. It is the highlight of my week. At the conclusion of each service, I am given a reading from Helen Steiner Rice, a verse of scripture, and the thought for the day that I share. It is uncanny how what I have preached coincides directly with what I am given to read. It is as the old hymn says: the revelation of Jesus is there "just when I need him most."

Fourth, supplication is when I intercede with God for others. I join Jesus in the work of going beyond human accomplishment. Healing, deliverance, and right thinking are possible to him who believes and has built up that belief so that it can benefit and bless others.

The primary supplication is for a debt free life. Being debt free from blame and owing forgiveness is number one. It means debt free financially, too. If I make supplication to God, I am taking responsibility for my whole life. I am including God in everything I am doing, and I am committing myself to ask God to let me be included in everything God is doing.

Fifth, stations are the places I ask God to reveal to me where I will be able to influence the lives of others. One of those stations today is sitting here at the computer. Another station was in a visit to the hospital. Another station was the place where I got the oil changed in the car for Karen. The other station was standing in the kitchen when my daughter came home from school with her report card. Praying will open our spirit to the places we can bring life to others. When I pray these daily stations, I am just asking God to let me notice them while I am in them. I am praying not to be led into temptation but into opportunity.

Sixth, silence is to give God a chance to breakthrough. Usually, I stretch my body while I wait for God to stretch me. This is a time of breathing deeply and being attentive to what lies just ahead. I wait for the assurance of God's presence and deliverance. When God is good to go, hopefully, so am I.

Last, sending steps are the first handful of things God wants me to do when I arise from prayer. They are the first movement of my prayer taking its stand in real time.

To build up our faith, praying in the Holy Spirit is to cultivate a growing life with God. To build up our faith praying in the Holy Spirit is to go fully interactive with God in living our life. We are seeking to make sense of the landscape of our life. In this pursuit, we are going to God as quickly as we can in each circumstance.

Proverbs 3:5–6 says, "Trust in the Lord with all your heart and lean not on your own understanding. In all your ways acknowledge him and he shall direct your paths" (NKJV). This word for trust literally means run to consult God without hesitation; hightail it! Don't be one who substantiates himself. Do as the hymn *Stand up for Jesus* recommends:

> Stand up, stand up for Jesus; stand in his strength alone. The arm of flesh will fail you; ye dare not trust you own. Put on the gospel armor; each piece put on with prayer. Where duty calls or danger, be never wanting there.

Whenever you do the work of building something up, that includes building up your faith, there are two constants: repetition and resistance. This is why we see the disciples of Jesus coming several times to Jesus and asking him to teach them to pray. One of these episodes is in Luke 11. Pay close attention to the context Luke uses to frame this lesson on how to pray. Remember in the original Greek there were no chapter breaks, no paragraphs, and no punctuation to mark the end of a sentence. You judged when the breaks occurred by the context itself.

What's the big picture? What are the basics we need to consider as we build up our faith praying in the Holy Spirit? Number one: consider the parable of the Good Samaritan. It begins with an expert in the law who stood up to test Jesus. I only wish this expert had wanted to test the character of God like Abraham did in Genesis 18, proving how gracious and righteous God is. But, instead, the expert was trying to discredit Jesus. The expert asks a question:

> What must I do to inherit eternal life? [Jesus replied,] "What is written in the law? How do you read it?" The expert answered, Love the Lord your God with all your heart and with all your soul and with all your strength and with all your mind; and Love your neighbor as yourself. "You have answered correctly," Jesus replied. "Do this and you will live." But, he wanted to justify himself, so he asked Jesus, And who is my neighbor?
>
> Luke 10:25–29

The first function of prayer is to simplify our life; to pare it down until the bedrock of everything we do is motivated by our love for God and neighbor. Prayer calls us to forsake justifying ourselves and choose this "better" course of action. We are responsible for knowing this and acting accordingly. We cannot pray, "Father, hallowed by your name" without rooting our actions in love. This love, as illustrated by the parable, is not an excuse to justify our actions. Love is not saying, "I'm okay, you're okay." Love admits that we have terrible wounds that need healing. Love addresses the way we can be abused and taken advantage of. Love picks us up, takes us off of the wrong road, and sacrificially provides us a place to be restored.

Jesus implies that the expert and all of us are responsible for choosing love as the foundation on which everything else is done. Our betrayal embraces love through repentance. Our bias, rooted in love, becomes a belief that can change the world. Rooted in betrayal, our bias is just another opinion. You reap what you sow. Jesus says we know this and our praying helps us remember. You can't bring unity by sowing discord. You can't reap prosperity on borrowed money. You can't reap peace by mistrust. You can't reap wholeness apart from holiness. You can't justify yourself by blaming other people for what's wrong in your life. You are responsible.

Our faith, the Bible says, works by love. Root our faith in anything else and it will be dysfunctional. It will be a distortion. I once served a church I called the "groundhog" church. I called it that because every time anyone raised their head up with something new, they got shot down. You learned to keep your head in the hole—head down and mouth shut.

I didn't fully realize the root of the problem until my last Sunday there. As I walked down the aisle toward the door, an older lady stuck out her hand to me in a final farewell. As I grasped her hand, she looked at me and said, "Preacher, when you get to Virginia, don't you expect those folks to love you because you are their pastor. You are going to have to earn their love."

This brings us back to the importance of praying: constantly turning, trusting, and talking with God. As Luke frames our teaching on prayer, we know love cannot be sown by force or as a requirement of law. It is built up in friendship with God. As we pray "Your kingdom come," we can be bold to ask, seek, and knock for whatever we need.

Jesus told his disciples to ask anything in his name, and it would be done for them. I was recently feeling deflated and discouraged. Immediately, I asked God to send someone to encourage me. A few minutes later my administrative assistant called and told me someone wanted to schedule a get-to-know-one-another visit for that evening prior to choir practice. I agreed. It was the best, most encouraging hour I had shared with anyone for a long time.

Don't be bashful or afraid to pray. You have an enemy. You are not it. When we pray "Give us each day our daily bread," we are reminded God will provide and prescribe for us what we need today. This is our confidence. The character of God will always prove greater than our conditions. This is our confidence even in the fight of our lives.

What is fear but believing a lie that our conditions are too much for the character of God? What is guilt but believing a lie that our lack of character is so deficient that God's character can't fill it? What is blame but believing a lie that people, ordinary sinners like you and me, should be expected to conduct themselves as God, always doing what is right? When we pray "Forgive us our sins for we also forgive everyone who sins against us," we understand that God calls us not only to be blessed but to be a blessing.

To build up your most holy faith is to take responsibility for your life. The opposite of this is to be irresponsible. Nature abhors a vacuum. So does our soul. That's why the opposite of building up your most holy faith is blame. When Adam was first challenged and had his faith perspective questioned by God, Adam points the finger at Eve. He doesn't see the error of his own ways. He is only able to see the error of others. The betrayal of sin brings on blindness: an unconscious bias that is positive towards ourselves and generally negative towards others, especially others who don't *see* things the way we do.

Blame makes us accusers—a particularly devilish moniker—those that affix blame or faults to others of which we are amazingly innocent. Insert tongue in cheek. The most recent example of this was a program on Link TV, *There You Go Again: George Orwell Comes to America.* On the program, experts from various fields talked about the ways in which George Orwell's writings on propaganda and language are relevant and expressed in today's political culture.

As I watched the program, the panelists shared how the manipulation of language and unconscious frames of reference channel us down a dark path. One expert shared in particular that we are "blind" to our own frames of reference, that ninety-eight percent of what we communicate is unconscious. But then he proceeded to list illustration after illustration of how "the other side" consciously is culpable for the way it frames the debate.

Which is it? What has this got to do with prayer? Everything! We are creatures of habit, most often blind habits. We are creatures who resist confessing or owning the specific ways we are rooted in sin. This is why we run to Jesus and ask him to teach us to pray. Lord, teach us how to build up our most holy faith. Lord, teach us how to take responsibility for our life. Lord, teach us to forgive.

In Luke 11:29–32, Jesus says there is a new sign we observe as we travel the road ahead. It is the sign of Jonah. When we pray "Forgive us our sins for we also forgive everyone who sins against us," we are admitting the singular sign that directs our actions from this day forward is the resurrection of Jesus Christ—the sign of Jonah.

Let this recalcitrant prophet teach us one of life's most important lessons. We sometimes have to die, be buried in the belly of the fish, and be resurrected before we arrive in the right place. This experience may have to happen multiple times before we move up the straight and narrow all by ourselves.

Most of us need practice at forgiving one another. Most of us didn't see it modeled for us as we grew up. It's something we have to practice. It may prove very uncomfortable. I remember once when I had spoken inappropriately about someone and went to their house to apologize and ask their forgiveness. I knocked on the door. They answered, and when they recognized it was me at the door—the vile offender—I tried to hurriedly apologize and ask for forgiveness. I blurted out, "I am sorry…" They agreed and slammed the door in my face.

Don't give up. The hurts we inflict and receive are real. Pray for the reality of the resurrection to take precedent over everything else. Allow the practice of praying and forgiving to focus your spiritual sight on the progress you are making with God.

We pray "And lead us not into temptation," so God can be the one Lord and leader for the course of action we take. We are not justifying ourselves as the expert in the law wanted to do. We are not trying to get even. We do not have the appropriate skill to be masters of the universe.

This is why in Matthew's Gospel Jesus finishes his model prayer with the phrase "Deliver us from evil." In Luke we are encouraged to pray and ask for the gift of the Holy Spirit. It is the revealing presence of the Holy Spirit in prayer that delivers us from falling captive to evil.

We are seeking to be moving at the speed of grace. God knows we need a method of training to keep in step with the Spirit. As you build up your faith, God says the best exercise for achieving fitness is prayer. Through prayer you are in union with God in taking responsibility for your life. Through prayer, you are verifying daily, moment by moment, that your faith is working. Jude says praying, empowered by the Holy Spirit, is the chief practice that accomplishes this purpose.

Why praying? Why not reading scripture? Why not meditation? Why not acts of kindness? By definition, prayer excels the others because prayer implies a submission or alignment of our will to God's. To pray is to literally *kneel toward*. Thus, praying is an outward sign of an inward allegiance and connection to God.

This is why praying in the name of Jesus is significant. The word and name of Jesus is your key to accessing the power and authority of God's kingdom on earth as it is in heaven. Bible study can reveal that same authority, but praying will give us access to it.

Go ahead. Ask God for the Holy Spirit, the Spirit of Jesus. Build up your most holy faith. Pray. Remember to maintain proper form as you repeat this spiritual exercise. Follow the pattern Jesus has given us but get to it. Build up your most holy faith praying in the Holy Spirit!

SMALL GROUP DISCUSSION QUESTIONS

1. What is your spiritual exercise of prayer like at this time?

2. How can you improve it in order to have a deeper and stronger connection with God?

3. Use the Seven S's for a time of group prayer.

4. Share with your group whether this outline helped you to focus better on communicating with God.

PRAYING IN THE POWER OF THE HOLY SPIRIT

When you pray, do you consciously access the all sufficiency of God's grace? Do you expect the serendipitous supervision of God? Have you remembered to use the Lord's Prayer as the pattern that marks your progress and maturity in prayer?

How does your style of praying match up to the Lord's Prayer? Think about the unresolved and unanswered prayers you have prayed over a long period. What's the hold up? What are the limiting behaviors and beliefs that have kept you praying the same prayers in the same way? What needs to change, the style or the substance?

When you pray, do you see yourself as more of a hatchling

breaking through to a new life or a bird or chick that's waiting for God to break the shell for you?

Let's review. We begin in repentance aligning ourselves with Jesus accompanying us along the Way. We choose to entrust our lives to Jesus. We believe and exchange following the blindness of our own bias for living in the light of God's word. We prepare for the journey ahead and build up our most holy faith, as Jude tells us, praying in the power of the Holy Spirit. In this way we keep ourselves in God's love as we wait for the mercy of our Lord Jesus Christ to bring us to eternal life. We build ourselves up in our most holy faith. We keep ourselves in God's love in the way of prayer.

John Wesley, the founder of Methodism, listed several spiritual practices God works through to strengthen and confirm our faith. He calls these practices "means of grace," visible means through which God gives invisible grace. Wesley divides them into two groups: works of piety and works of charity. Out of all these ways of working, Jude tells us the way above all others that God uses to build up our most holy faith is the way of prayer.

What we are emphasizing here is the work of God to conform us into the image of his Son. I know I need practice in conforming to the image of Jesus. How about you? Do you need practice to pray like Jesus? Do you need practice to respond to situations in the same spirit as Jesus does? I have a sneaking suspicion you do almost as much as I do.

Golfing legend, Ben Hogan says the point of all practice is improvement. But, as my preaching professor in seminary told me, practice doesn't make perfect. Practice makes permanent. Only perfect practice makes perfect. That's why this chapter refocuses our attention on the Lord's Prayer. Look with me at the Lord's Prayer and how it follows the same path that God uses when he is at work in us, his pathway of grace.

When we think of the Lord's Prayer, too often we think of it as something we can just quickly repeat or something that is said in unison on Sunday morning, but it is the model that Jesus gives to form all of our praying. He said after this pattern and manner we are to pray:

Our Father in heaven, hallowed be your name, your kingdom come, your will be done on earth as it is in heaven. Give us today our daily bread. Forgive us our debts, as we also have forgiven our debtors. And lead us not into temptation, but deliver us from the evil one.

Matthew 6:9–13

We find this prayer in the midst of the Sermon on the Mount. Before Jesus begins this outline for prayer, he tells us the things to which we need to attend.

Number one, Jesus says we need to know how we are going to share our lives. I am not asking for the items on your daily planner. I am asking, "How will we fulfill our vocations as followers of Jesus today?" I'm not talking about making a list of what you're going to give to Goodwill. Jesus says he wants you to know how to share your life so that God can be the one who commends you and rewards you, so you don't call attention to yourself, but to God and how you are becoming stronger. Often when folks in the world become stronger they advertise it. If they grow stronger physically, of course they can always flex their muscles. When they become stronger mentally, they can show off their degrees. When they become published and recognized, they can go on all of the talk shows.

God says when you share or serve, the primary person who should be noticed or praised for your sharing is God himself. Jesus warns us against saying we do things because we are inspired when we are really trying to be noticed for our own initiative.

The Lord doesn't want us just to repeat endless repetitions of words or phrases and then think, *I've said my prayers. I should get what I want and need right now. Thank you Lord.* We also don't want to make the mistake of acting as if prayer is unnecessary. I have known someone who felt this way. He didn't think he needed to pray. God knew what he needed and God could read his mind, so he didn't need to spend a lot of time praying or asking God stuff that God already knew.

The scripture might hint at that mindset because it counsels against repetition but Jesus is inviting us to a deeply personal and interactive experience in prayer. He says don't be like those who mindlessly enunciate syllables and expect to get heard. You wouldn't carry on a conversation like that with anyone else. Jesus says your Father knows what you need before you ask him (Matthew 6:8). But, that doesn't cancel out the asking. As soon as Jesus says don't ramble on and on in vain repetition, he begins to give you a pattern for how you are to pray.

There is a very good reason praying is so important. In the Judgment where all of us have to give an account for our lives, God will never say to you, depart from me, you never knew enough about me to enter into heaven. On the other hand, every time Jesus speaks of judgment he usually ends it with "Depart from me, I never knew you." God says it is not so much about us knowing him, as it is about us allowing God to know our hearts. God wants to enter into a relationship with us that makes the difference.

This is why repentance comes first in the pathway of grace. This is why our faith in Jesus is to be built up through prayer. We cannot play the role of the victim. We cannot allow ourselves to get stuck blaming others for where we are. We cannot say, "There's nothing I can do about the way things are in my life."

God says, "Yes, there is. There is a lot you can do. You can build up your most holy faith, praying in the power of the Holy Spirit. You can pray believing and you shall have what you ask."

God wants us to enter into a relationship of prayer with him so that there is nothing, absolutely nothing, that is impossible to us, but all things are possible to him who believes and offers that faith up to God in prayer.

Look again at the context in which God's pattern for prayer is given. It is set between a lesson on knowing how to give and a lesson on how to fast: how to do without anything except the opportunity to seek God's kingdom and its righteousness first. Prayer is the rock solid center of living.

The reason why prayer is so important is because God wants to enter into a deep and intimate relationship with you. The only way I know to bring it to light and to illustrate it is the way in which Adam Hamilton, pastor of the Church of the Resurrection in Leawood, Kansas, described it one time. He said he was going to a conference and his family went with him. In particular his teenage daughter went with him to this conference. They also had a youth rally as a part of this conference, and his daughter had met a young man who she liked. She asked her daddy, Adam Hamilton, "Daddy, could I walk with him on the beach this evening?"

He agreed with the stipulation that he walk with them. Now he didn't have to go side by side. He and his daughter negotiated, and he walked about twenty to thirty yards behind them. Hamilton said it was one of the most excruciating times of his life because he was jealous of that young boy. The young man was with his daughter walking down the beach, basically a total stranger. Yet, they were sharing, talking, laughing, leaning over, and whispering. He said at that point in her life if he had called her name, she might answer in one word, usually either very abruptly as if she was being offended to have her name spoken.

Hamilton said, "We were walking up the beach, and there she was having the best time talking to this person, getting to know him. I wanted her to talk to me like that." He said they finished the evening and walked the young man back to his hotel. Then he asked a favor of his daughter. He asked her if she would walk on the beach with him. She finally agreed, and he shared with her how he was glad she could walk with the young boy but wished for the same. He wanted her to remember how much he loved her and how much he wanted to talk to her, too.

That is the heart of a father; I know, it is like myself. I have a daughter who is a young teenage girl, and I love her. I know her. I want her to want me to know her, to open her heart to her daddy and tell me what is going on and to let me hear her say it rather than the one word response I get when I call her name. I would like to be the boy on the telephone who she can talk to for hours at a time. God says the very same thing. I want a relationship with you where I can get to know you. If you will let me know your heart, I'm going to let you know mine. Everything together is working for your benefit when you love me and let me love you.

God calls us to prayer as the chief way of building ourselves up in our most holy faith, of being strong in God's power and God's might. Getting to know God and, more importantly, allowing God to know our heart is our life and strength. Giving God open access to our heart and being in a relationship with him through Christ is why God calls us to pray.

Jesus starts our open-access-to-God training with these words. "Our Father in heaven, hallowed be your name" (Matthew 6:9). The prayer begins as God's way begins: as a basic call to repentance, a call to align ourselves with God. The only way we can do that is for the Father to become Our Father.

When Jesus went to the cross, he was basically saying it is not enough. It is not enough for us to be made in God's image because that image has been marred. We have all sinned and fallen short of the glory of God. I want you to notice whose place Jesus took on the cross. I don't know if you have ever really paid attention to it or not. I am not speaking metaphorically or in a representative way. I am asking you to pay attention to the name of the actual person for whom Jesus served as a substitute. The man's name was Barrabus. Barrabus means "*a* son of *a* father." *The* son of *the* Father wants us to be like his Son.

The call of God is sown into our hearts to foster and fulfill this longing to be a child of God. And whoever God calls, he foreknew. God knows the difference faith will make in our lives, and he wants us to have a substantial faith in him. He knows what our lives will look like when we put our trust in him. But whoever God foreknew he predestined to be conformed into the image of his son.

God wants us to pray because he wants to transform each one of us from a Barrabus to Jesus. He wants us to be changed from a son or daughter of a father to a son or daughter of the Most High God. He wants to transform every one of us from a murderer to becoming a giver of life. He wants to transform us from being a Barrabus into a Jesus.

He calls us to pray this way. "Our Father in heaven, hallowed be your name." Lord let me revere you. Let me respect you. Let me fear you, and let me humble myself before you. Let me align myself with your way. Let me accompany you in whatever you want to do. Let me be a part of your family. Adopt me, and let me become one of your precious children.

God will do that, and God will honor that prayer. Jesus outlines it for us. God says, "Come and align your life with mine. Humbly repent. Reverence me as one who can call me their own father. But I want you to exercise your faith." You meet the resistance of your mind and life's tests and challenges by saying, "God, your will be done. Your kingdom come, on earth as it is in heaven."

So what we are praying is this: God let everything that I am thinking that is earthbound or limited by my experience or the opinion of others be exchanged for the way your kingdom works. I exchange the way my will works for the way your will works, for the way your power is demonstrated.

I don't know about you, but I am like a lot of people. I have made some dumb choices when it comes to how I spent my money or how much I spent when I didn't have it. We have accumulated debt, and we are working on being debt free now. I could thank a lot of people for that.

One of the things I saw this year is that in times past we have tried to get out of debt by just paying what we could. It almost felt like I was scrounging around for fill dirt for all of the holes I have dug, and this year I wanted it to be different. I wanted to build mountains so that even if the mountains were leveled, all my holes would be filled in, and I could make a new start and overcome all the dumb things I have done in the past.

I wanted encouragement. I wanted to try to find the faith to do that. I was reading Revelation 22 about how it was going to be in the new heaven and the new earth. I wanted to know how it was going to be in God's kingdom. It says the tree of life is there, and it produces fruit—new fruit, a new crop, a full crop of fruit, different kinds of fruit every single month. They have harvest time in the kingdom every month. I am thinking we usually have it once a year. For some of us the harvest time is every other week or every month when we get paid. I said, "Man it would be nice to have a harvest every month instead of once a year."

But, listen to Jesus as he teaches in Mark, chapter four. He tells a parable about the soils. The last variety of soil Jesus describes is good ground. He says good ground is able to produce "some thirty fold, some sixty fold, and some a hundred fold" (Mark 4:8, 20) Remember the kingdom pattern—a harvest every month. A thirty fold increase would translate into something productive every day. A sixty fold production model would be beneficial twice a day. A hundred fold return would be receiving an increase three times each day. Certainly, with the ability afforded to us by the Internet and other technologies, this is not out of reach.

I began to pray and ask God, "Lord how is it that I could work and be obedient to you and produce that much each month? How could I work and instead of putting my money in a savings account making 2 percent a year, increase my productivity to match the possibilities of good soil in the kingdom of God? Is that possible God?"

God showed me that it was possible. I have got to learn a whole lot before it becomes likely. His will be done, his kingdom come. Some of you are thinking, *Well Norm, you're crazy. It is not going to work like that. It is too much to ask.* Well, let's just say I asked for it and only get halfway; I think I'll still be doing pretty well.

We want our faith to be exchanged. We let go of all our predetermined limits. Turn around and say to God, "I want to represent your kingdom, its power, and multiplying ability to be fruitful. We want to move forward to the way you want us to be." In the kingdom there is no prejudice. In the kingdom there is no fear. In the kingdom there is no worry. In the kingdom there is no opinion forced on other people, no coercion. We want things to be done. We want to operate on the earth as it is in the kingdom.

We certainly want to do as the prophet said: "to act justly, and to love mercy and to walk humbly with God" (Micah 6:8). This is our calling, to love one another as Jesus has given us commandment. We pray for our faith to not just be a "pie in the sky" kind of thing, but to be realized faith, to be faith that works by love that makes a difference in people's lives. It makes a difference in us, in our character, integrity, patience, and kindness.

We also pray, "Give us today our daily bread." This again emphasizes the importance of prayer and the reason why we ask. This verse literally means we are asking God to prescribe for us, as the Great Physician, exactly what we need today. We are asking God to give us what we need to face the difficulties and the heartaches, and for the strength to forgive and to be responsible for the things we need to do. We are asking God to teach us how to let go of the hurts that will come our way. And we are asking him to teach us how to not hold onto some of the words that we hear, but how to move in wholeness and wellness in spirit, soul, and body.

I hope you'll remember the illustration of a father's heart when I told you how much fathers long to talk with their children, not just talk to or try to read the mind of their children. They want their children to actively engage them and to ask questions of them and to seek their wisdom and counsel.

Here is another reason why we are called to pray and how it proves to be the best way we can build up our faith. When we recognize we need something, the doctor doesn't pass us on the way to his office and say, "Man that person is sick. I need to recruit them to come to my office." Likewise, the pharmacist doesn't go to work at the drugstore and say, "Man, Norm is sick today. I am going to call him and tell him I have already prescribed something for him. I will tell him he doesn't have to pick it up. I will bring it to him on the way home." If pharmacists started to independently prescribe medicine for patients who hadn't come to them for medicine, they wouldn't be in business very long. We would say they are doing things illegally and unethically to be writing prescriptions that weren't prescribed.

In the same way, God really wants us to offer him our prayers, to come to him and say, "Lord, I know the shape I am in. I am asking you to prescribe for me what I need today, and I will follow your direction. I will trust you." So we pray that we might be ready to be so fed by God, led by God, and provided for by God, that we can be ready to even offer the ultimate blessing, the blessing of forgiveness. Forgive us Lord as we forgive those who trespass against us.

I was asked once about a preacher who had fallen into sin. My only comment was, "I don't need any help falling, but I do need help to stand. So let's pray for the person rather than condemn the person." Sure, I wanted the preacher to be accountable, to repent and turn away from sin. However, I also wanted the preacher to serve a while without being under the spotlight and to mature to a place the preacher wouldn't sin again. So, we don't need any help falling.

God says we can fall out of his favor and out of the way by withholding forgiveness. Did you know that every act of blame and withholding forgiveness is based on a lie? I am not saying that there aren't real hurts, real abuse, and real wrong that is done to a person, but forgiveness is not saying things were okay. Forgiveness is saying things were beyond terrible, but I will not make you pay myself. If some things are done publicly, you will have to pay publicly.

If somebody says something to me privately that hurts and I forgive the person, that doesn't mean the person didn't say hurtful things. It means I will not allow those words to define who I am. I will not let what comes from the outside defile me. Jesus said the only way something on the outside can do that is if you let it in. If you withhold forgiveness in your heart, it is basically letting it in.

I told a person once while teaching on forgiveness to "rinse and repeat with the Word of God in your life until you are clean and you're forgiven because you have forgiven others."

Forgive us Lord as we forgive those who trespass against us. Don't let me fall trapped to the lie that expects everybody to be perfect, to be like God, knowing good and evil, knowing right and wrong and acting right all of the time. It is an impossible standard, so I am not going to hold them to an impossible standard. I know you forgive me. You remember that I am dust. You help me remember that others are dust like me, too. We are all dusty. We all need to have the cleansing of forgiveness applied to us. We thank you that you do.

Nothing weakens us like blame or withholding forgiveness. Withholding forgiveness is placing blame and leaving it as it is. Whether that blame is directed toward others or ourselves, we are sapped of strength. It doesn't matter where the drain is located. The water still leaves the sink.

I have weakened myself countless times, my dreams unrealized, because of the sapping nature of blame. A couple of years ago I was committed to being fit, losing weight, and operating at peak faithfulness. God had called me to weigh 170 pounds. June 1 of that year I carried 210 pounds on this 5-foot 10-inch frame—too much. By August 1 I was well on my way, down to 178 pounds, eating healthier and exercising regularly.

Then on August 3 I woke up in the night with a fever. I was acting as chaplain at Camp Alta Mons, a Christian camp near our home. I thought to get through the morning at camp then go home, get a good nap, get over what was bothering me, and then go back for vespers that night.

At lunchtime I came home from camp to rest. When I woke up from my nap, it was 7:00 p.m., and my temperature was 103°. I didn't go back for vespers. Other than going to the doctor that next morning, I slept through until Sunday evening, only waking to drink, eat, and go to the bathroom. I went back to the doctor on Monday and was told I was fighting e-coli bacteria. I have never felt so drained.

What proved more draining was the way I stopped pursuing my goal. I still had an appetite but very little energy. I didn't adjust. I didn't take small steps to compensate. I didn't really do anything but blame what had happened for sliding me back into my old lethargy and eating habits.

It has taken me these three years to come to grips with the actions I need to take, the adjustments I need to make, and the attitude I need to maintain. Even though I am still facing physical challenges, I have turned in a direction of becoming fit again. (If you want to see what I did during my Forty Days to Forty Pounds Challenge, you can request a copy of my journal for free at reverendnorm@msn.com.)

We pray "lead us not into temptation" because we are not to be limited by our failures but to learn from them. I hope you have learned that what separates a professional from an amateur is properly practicing what is essential consistently over time. This is why professionals do not jump into their seasons without coming to training camp first. All ball players go through the fundamentals. They pick up the signals that will keep them on the same page with the coach and the rest of the team. They rehearse their movements, so they know how to execute and make plays together.

Even an individual sport like golf calls for practicing your swing and the situations of a match repeatedly before a game. Playing just becomes public practice. In every swing we can see the golfer following the pathway of grace, and so too should every prayer. We begin with the proper stance: a reverent, expectant humility. We next check our grip. It is one of faith, firm but not too tight. Focus the hidden power of muscle and mind as you complete your backswing. From your core let the power gather speed until it reaches through your grip to the club as you make your downswing. The acceleration of your swing follows the straight and narrow path to make sweet contact with the ball. The ball is designed to fly but sits on the ground until your influence moves it to its appointed destiny. Your final act is following through, lifting up your head and seeing the glorious outcome of a shot well played.

Wow! What if that last paragraph described your prayer life? Some I know would be overjoyed if it just described their golf swing. But, I ask you to consider how God is at work in you to build up your most holy faith. Consider the last portion of the Lord's Prayer.

"Deliver us from evil." Let's stay on the golf course for a few more minutes to illustrate what this portion of our prayer life means. I am not a well-practiced golfer. I play a couple of times a year. I trust you would say I'm a pretty good golfer considering I never practice. I birdied the first hole the last time I played a round.

My final score will not be disclosed due to the fact it might incriminate me as a pretty pitiful golfer. I still hold the dubious record at the Hat Creek Golf Course for the most under par and over par in the same nine holes. Of course, that's not the way the score is kept. Anyone looking at the final score would have seen nine over for nine holes. They never would have known I was four under after four holes.

Your prayer life needs to be kept in perspective the same way. The evil one would want nothing better than for you to expect your prayers to have as much to do with luck as they do to the intimate and loving relationship you have with your Father who is in heaven. The evil one would like you to get a reputation as a pretty good Christian, considering you never practice.

To build up your most holy faith, praying in the Holy Spirit is to join God in taking responsibility for your life. To build up your faith is to practice making your faith both permanent and perfect. Building up your faith praying in the Holy Spirit is the launching pad for blessing. You are prepared for action. You have stepped up your game. You expect to hear your heavenly coach call you by name, saying, "_____, get in there!"

SMALL GROUP DISCUSSION QUESTIONS

1. In what ways would you explain your practice of prayer? To yourself? To others? To God?

2. How does your prayer life prepare you for living and for blessing others?

3. Using the golf swing analogy, which of the following most often describes the outcomes of your prayers? *I hit the sweet spot with that one. I topped that one. I hooked that badly enough. I pushed that one off.*

4. What element of your practice of prayer needs the most attention?

Bless

The Lord said to Moses, "Tell Aaron and his sons, This is how you are to bless the Israelites. Say to them: 'The Lord bless you and keep you; the Lord make his face to shine upon you and be gracious to you; The Lord turn his face toward you and give you peace.'"

Numbers 6:22–26

Rejoice in the Lord always. I will say it again: Rejoice! Let your gentleness [appropriateness] be evident to all. The Lord is near. Do not be anxious about anything, but in everything by prayer and petition, with thanksgiving, present your requests to [verify

your requests with] God. And the peace of God, which transcends all understanding, will guard [serve as an advance guard to] your hearts and minds in Christ Jesus.

Philippians 4:4–7

When a man is wrapped up in himself, he makes a pretty small package.

—John Ruskin

MOVED BY THE SPIRIT BEYOND MYSELF

Faith works by love. Praying in the Holy Spirit examines us to see if that is true. Blessing is expressing that faith in love. It is bringing others to worship God and give thanks to God. Blessing sees the big picture of the kingdom of God. Blessing is practical in its kindness. Blessing is not about calling attention to itself. Blessing is about others, but it's more than just hot air or empty activity. Blessing does not do good by evil means. The ends do not justify the means because blessing is not rooted in force but faith, not in compulsion but compassion. Blessing will die rather than reach a desired outcome outside of the Holy Spirit's leadership.

Look at Jesus in the garden of Gethsemane. The words he speaks in the garden show Jesus is just as ready to wait on God as to work for God. Jesus prayed, "Not my will, but yours be done" (Matthew 26:39, 42, 44). Three times Jesus perseveres in agonizing prayer to make sure God's will is done. Three times he finds his disciples sleeping and drowsy, unable to keep up with him. The only rest Jesus had was to know the will of God for his next steps. What about you and me?

Jesus was the incarnate blessing of God. He never became frantic or hurried. He was always timely. He waited thirty years to start his ministry. He did this not only to fulfill traditional expectations for a prophetic ministry but also to be a sign to those of us today who claim success comes by being the quickest or youngest to take advantage of our opportunities instead through obedience to God.

Early success or early failure carries a risk of being drawn into bitterness. Bitterness is the strategy of a survivalist. You can only do what you are doing.

Blessing is an expression of obedience. "We love because he first loved us," and we bless because he first blessed us (1 John 4:19). We are moved forward to live out of God's strength when we live a life of blessing.

Once, two brothers came over to help us cut tobacco. Their father said they were good workers. And they were energetic. For those who are unfamiliar with the skill required for cutting tobacco, you are handling a very sharp knife. With it, you are splitting a stalk a little more than an inch in diameter. You guide the knife, split the stalk about three-fourths of the way down, and then bend over and cut off the stalk at the base. You then turn the tobacco plant upside down and slide it onto a tobacco stick. This procedure should take about ten to fifteen seconds. The key is to do it quickly and repetitively without cutting off or breaking off any leaves.

My father was the most efficient farmer I ever saw perform this skill. Six plants per stick, Daddy could cut over 300 sticks per day by himself. Each plant had an average of fifteen leaves. That's 27,000 chances to cut off a leaf in an average day. I doubt if Daddy ever cut off twenty-seven in one day.

But these brothers were not Daddy. They jumped into the work with much more confidence than skill. They seemed to be able to cut off a leaf or leaves on every stalk. Every time they bent over to cut off the base of the stalk, you heard more crunching and snapping. Then, we watched in horror as they rammed the stalk onto the tobacco stick, impaling even more leaves.

The first ten minutes of their "help" was agonizing. The next ten minutes were filled with furtive glances from one member of our family to the other with imploring eyes as to what should be done. Ten minutes more and Daddy called for a break.

We pulled the refreshments out of the shade, and Daddy pulled the two brothers aside and thanked them for helping us "catch up" to where we needed to be. Daddy paid them extra, I think to make sure they went home. We were not blessed.

Blessing does not arise out of doing for others because you like doing what is good. This is especially true when the emphasis is on what *you like.* You always have to be mindful of how your actions affect others. I'm sure you've heard the story of *Goldilocks and the Three Bears,* but I'll retell the fairy tale as a review.

Once upon a time, there was a little girl named Goldilocks. She went for a walk in the forest. Pretty soon, she came upon a house. She knocked, and when no one answered, she walked right in.

At the table in the kitchen, there were three bowls of porridge. Goldilocks was hungry. She tasted the porridge from the first bowl. "This porridge is too hot!" she exclaimed. So, she tasted the porridge from the second bowl. "This porridge is too cold," she said. So, she tasted the last bowl of porridge. "Ahhh, this porridge is just right," she said happily, and she ate it all up.

After she'd eaten the three bears' breakfasts, she decided she was feeling a little tired. So, she walked into the living room where she saw three chairs. Goldilocks sat in the first chair to rest her feet. "This chair is too big!" she exclaimed. So she sat in the second chair. "This chair is too big, too!" she whined. So she tried the last and smallest chair. "Ahhh, this chair is just right," she sighed. But just as she settled down into the chair to rest, it broke into pieces!

Goldilocks was very tired by this time, so she went upstairs to the bedroom. She lay down in the first bed, but it was too hard. Then she lay in the second bed, but it was too soft. Then she lay down in the third bed, and it was just right. Goldilocks fell asleep.

As she was sleeping, the three bears came home. "Someone's been eating my porridge," growled the Papa bear. "Someone's been eating my porridge," said the Mama bear. "Someone's been eating my porridge, and they ate it all up!" cried the Baby bear. "Someone's been sitting in my chair," growled the Papa bear. "Someone's been sitting in my chair," said the Mama bear. "Someone's been sitting in my chair, and they've broken it all to pieces," cried the Baby bear.

They decided to look around some more, and when they got upstairs to the bedroom, Papa bear growled, "Someone's been sleeping in my bed." "Someone's been sleeping in my bed, too," said the Mama bear. "Someone's been sleeping in my bed, and she's still there!" exclaimed Baby bear.

Just then, Goldilocks woke up and saw the three bears. She screamed, "Help!" And she jumped up and ran out of the room. Goldilocks ran down the stairs, opened the door, and ran away into the forest. And she never returned to the home of the three bears.

Blessing does not arise to satisfy how we feel. Blessing is not a *quid pro quo* agreement. I'll scratch your back if you'll scratch mine. Just as finding porridge or an empty chair or a comfortable bed does not mean it is necessarily ours to enjoy, finding a need doesn't mean we necessarily fill it. Every blessing offered is given in response to need. But, every need does not demand a blessing from us. We would be quickly burned out and of no help at all if we operated that way. Every blessing offered is given in response to need, but it is because the Holy Spirit moves in response to need. We need to be moved by the Holy Spirit.

Problems arise if we are not led by the Holy Spirit. One of those problems is that we will simply overlook the need. I don't know about you, but I can get in the zone and have no clue what's going on sometimes. An example is when Karen and I were traveling one winter day, and she told me to watch the ice on the road ahead. I did. Our car stayed straight. We had no shimmying, no fishtailing. The crossing of the icy patch was picture perfect. I only failed to notice one other thing.

"Norm," Karen said, "Did you see that red light you just ran through?"

I had to reply, "No."

"I thought so," she said.

Maybe you're not that oblivious. We've got errands to run, projects to complete, deadlines to meet, and we're just occupied with our stuff. Wake up. Pay attention. Remember, in the midst of everything God wants to say to you as he did to Abraham, "I will make you a blessing."

Another problem that arises out of not being led by the Holy Spirit is being overwhelmed by the need. Study the ministry of Jesus. You see him tired but never overwhelmed. The moment he is called to do something outside of the direct leadership of the Holy Spirit, he moves immediately back to building up his faith in prayer. In Luke 4, Jesus teaches in the synagogue, casts out a demonic spirit, rebukes the fever out of Simon Peter's mother-in-law, and has people lined up at the door waiting for his touch to heal or deliver them.

The next morning before the line forms again, Jesus finds a solitary place of prayer. There he clarifies and determines what will occupy his attention that day. Even when the people find him and try to persuade him to bless them as he had others, Jesus knows what he must do.

In John 4, Jesus had to go through Samaria and have a divine appointment with a woman at the well. In Mark 10, amidst a great throng of people, Jesus hears the one voice of blind Bartimaeus. John 5 tells of Jesus healing a man beside the pool of Bethesda. Why this man instead of the thousands of others who were there in the time of the Feast? Why? The Apostle Peter tells in Acts 10:38, it is because Jesus was anointed with the full measure of the Holy Spirit.

When we operate outside of that same anointing, it is easy to face another problem: finding ourselves overmatched. I've always wanted to be successful financially. But I come from a long line of folks who wanted to be something but decided for one reason or another they were overmatched. Circumstances being what they are, I am the way I am. But the Apostle Paul says, "I am what I am by the grace of God."

Jesus knew we could easily find ourselves overwhelmed and overmatched. This is why he led his disciples by saying, "Do not be afraid." I have heard God speak to me that way. Every time, God is promising to be with me to make the difference I have said I cannot make by myself.

There will be some things, without the direction of the Holy Spirit, we would not even consider. Instead we would say, "I'm too shy … I have too much of this … I have too little of that … I could never do that. I would like to do your will, but it's above my pay grade."

Second Corinthians 5:17–19 says:

> If anyone is in Christ, he is a new creation; the old has gone, the new has come! All this is from God, who reconciled us to himself through Christ and gave us the ministry of reconciliation: that God was reconciling the world to himself in Christ, not counting men's sins against them. And he has committed to us the message of reconciliation.

Blessing reminds us our reconciliation to God in Jesus is greater than our reconciliation to our circumstances. We are not overmatched because God is not overmatched. But let's say we jump into blessing others. We are bold, some say crazy. We face a different problem, one of overreaching. Ever said too much? Ever overstayed your welcome? Ever been inappropriate? There are two reasons why we allow for overreaching people: sincerity and solidarity. Want to be Goldilocks? You are sincerely hungry. You are sincerely tired. Never mind the fact that you are trespassing. You mean well. You have good, maybe even great ideas. The imposition is worth it. After all, you're sincere. It doesn't matter if your ideas have been tried and reaped havoc before. Your intentions are purer. You are sincere.

Jesus was sincerely hungry in the wilderness, but he didn't bless himself when it went against God's Word. Stretching or shading the truth is a sure sign you've been pinned by the problem of overreaching.

The other reason overreaching people are allowed to operate is that we find ourselves in solidarity with their goals. Ever watch a football game when a receiver has trapped the ball and they scoop it up and try to sell an incompletion as a reception? Did you see their teammates running to the referee to say, "He didn't catch it, Mr.

Ref."? I know you would never go into your employer's register and take money out for yourself, but would you go along with the state doing by force what you can't do in good faith?

Standards of conduct become less substantial than achieving desired outcomes when we overreach. Cheating is allowed. The rule of law gives way to the rule of what I like. Principles are determined by preferences. Don't ask for the details. That would only delay what we know we should do. This is not the spirit of blessing. This is the spirit of lawlessness.

We were meant for blessing. God calls us to bless. Let's look at a story in the scripture where God's call to bless overcame all of these problems. It is a familiar passage in Luke 2. Check out the shepherds who were keeping watch over their flocks that first Christmas night. Angels appeared. A whole host of them showed up. They set the sky ablaze. They sang. They heralded a message from heaven. They came in such a way that they could not be overlooked. "The glory of the Lord shone round about them" (v.9). The shepherds were not allowed to be overwhelmed. The news was just too good. "Do not be afraid. I bring you good news of great joy that will be for all the people. Today in the town of David a Savior has been born to you; he is Christ the Lord" (v.10). They were given a sign that was easy to understand and follow so that they didn't feel overmatched. "This shall be a sign to you: You will find the baby wrapped in cloths and lying in a manger" (v.12).

Finally, hear the testimony of the shepherds. They never called attention to their experience with the angels. Their story was about what God was doing. No shepherd tried to work out a book deal. No one was invited to go back out to the hills and wait for the next angelic appearance. They said, "Let's go see this thing which has happened which the Lord has made known unto us" (v. 15). "When they had seen him, they spread the word concerning what had been told them about this child" (v. 17). They demonstrated complete transparency. They had no hidden agenda. They had good news to share. It was the same good news God had shared with them.

They didn't overreach. The scripture says they returned to their responsibilities, "glorifying and praising God" (v. 20). Their life, their words had become an overlay of God's life and words. There was no difference between the two. They were into what God was doing. God was into what they were doing.

This is the life of blessing. Our story and God's are one.

So the real question is, "How do I decide what I should do in any given situation?" First, let's distinguish between chores and seasonal work. Growing up on the farm that's how our work was categorized.

We had daily chores. We fed the hogs. We fed the chickens. We fed the dog and cats. Daddy did the milking. My grandmother churned the butter. You know this kind of routine. You take out the garbage. You wash the dishes. You go to work. You clock in. Stuff has to be done. The Bible says, "Anyone, then, who knows the good he ought to do and doesn't do it, sins" (James 4:17). It also says, "If a man shall not work, he shall not eat" (2 Thessalonians 3:10). Sometimes, work just needs to be done. So, we do it!

My hope is that you determine who does the chores out of love. Chores aren't assigned to others because you don't want to do them. Chores are assigned to teach responsibility. In fulfilling our obligation to love one another, chores call us to see our part in things. Chores demonstrate our trust. Chores teach us self-care is the prerequisite for the care of others. Brush your teeth. Wash your hands. Pick up after yourself. This is why building up our most holy faith praying in the Holy Spirit is the prerequisite for blessing. The Bible says we love others as we love ourselves.

Beyond our required chores, we had seasonal work. The chief difference between the two was that chores were assumed things we did everyday, while Daddy assigned seasonal work to us. As we grew older Daddy wanted us to recognize what needed to be done. He wanted us to know the way he did things so well we would go ahead and tend to things. I'm afraid we fell short of that expectation. When, how, and to what extent should other work be done? We didn't seem to know. Sometimes it seems we ask the question our whole lives. How do I determine when it is the season or moment to join God in a particular activity?

This is what the call to bless reveals. God speaks. We respond. God whispers. We move. God informs. We act. God leads. We dance. God initiates. We follow. God corrects. We change. God calls. We bless.

SMALL GROUP DISCUSSION QUESTIONS:

1. Discuss with your group about how you think someone's life would look if he/she fully lived being led by the Holy Spirit.

2. When you look back, can you see places where you overlooked a need?

3. Have there been times when you felt overwhelmed?

4. What do you think it means to "be into what God is doing?" How might this change the way you live each day?

THE PARABLE OF THE PANCAKE

Before anyone begins a life of service or sets out to bless someone, they should learn the parable of the pancake. I love pancakes. When my weight is not a problem, we have them almost every morning. When my weight is a problem, I long for the pancake season to return.

I grew up eating pancakes. My mama would fix them for us. I still follow her method when I fix them today. Mama began with flour. I begin with the pancake mix from Walmart®. Mama added an egg, buttermilk, and a touch of oil. I add water to the mix and a little oil to the pan. We both stir the ingredients to get a good semi-liquid batter. We both pour out the batter into the hot pan. We both watch over that soon-to-be-pancake. We wait until the heat has had its effect. Then, we turn the pancake over with the spatula. A few moments more and we decide the pancake is ready to serve. The pancake does not leave the pan of its own accord. The maker of the pancake moves the pancake.

We are like that pancake. We need to get out of our box. We need something added to our life. We need to be stirred up. We need to face the heat and wait to be turned. We need the maker to choose when we are to serve.

I recently bought pancake mix. It had the expiration date listed, so I knew I had plenty of time. I could have bacon and eggs, cereal, muffins, Pop-Tarts®, a breakfast casserole, and a host of other things before I ate pancakes again. Why? I knew the expiration date for my pancake mix. God says, "Now is the day of salvation" (2 Corinthians 6:2). Why? We don't know our own expiration date. Jesus insists we repent because unforeseen events occur. Accidents happen. Hebrews 9:27 says we are all destined to die once. But that appointment is not something we set up.

Just like the pancake mix, we don't jump into the shopping cart. Our future Maker must draw us from the shelf to the cart, pay for us, and give us a home. While the Maker is doing his work, we must be moved. Today, if you hear God's voice, do not put it off or ignore it in anyway. Turn to go with God. Follow Jesus. Repent. Move with your Maker! You might never know what you missed if you don't.

I used to make pancakes the old fashioned way. Everything was put together from scratch. Now, I have someone do that for me. When I get the mix out of its box now, I'm missing just one key ingredient—water. In our lives we can try to throw things together from scratch, but in reality there is only one key ingredient. The Apostle Peter says there are a lot of things you can add to this ingredient but without it you have a dried up mix of stuff.

I like my pancakes plain. When I fix pancakes for Karen or Hannah, I might add everything from pecans to chocolate chips, but without water in the mix nothing is held together. In the same way our spiritual life needs the key ingredient of faith. Without it nothing is held together. You can stir all you want to, and nothing will come together without faith. Ask your Maker to provide you with the Living Water of faith today.

Add water to your pancake mix, and there is hope you might have pancakes. Have faith in God, and there is hope you will have eternal life. You thought that was it? Faith alone is sufficient, right? Well sort of.

The pancake mix can never become a pancake without water, but the water must be stirred in and blended with the mix if you hope to have something good to eat. Faith too must be stirred into our lives. It can't float like a freestanding prop of some kind. It can't set under us like a crutch that helps us move along. The Holy Spirit must be integrated with our spirit. Our spirit bears witness with the Holy Spirit that we are God's through Jesus Christ. Jude says, "Build up your most holy faith, and pray in the Holy Spirit" (Jude 1:20). Mix yourself up with God. Get stirred up.

Otherwise, like the pancake we are a lumpy glob of mix and water. We are like the shoot that springs up from the soil with the promise of life but has no root to sustain it (Mark 4:5–6). Don't sell yourself or God short. Allow the Holy Spirit to stir you up. Ask God to baptize you with the Holy Spirit. Jesus pours the missing ingredient of faith into you, so once stirred you can be poured out to share faith with others. You don't want to be the unwanted glob of grace in someone's life. Get stirred up.

The pancake knows that if it got out of the box, water was added, and it was stirred up there is only one conclusion. It is about to be poured out. Likewise, when we get out of our box and begin a relationship with God, when faith is added and the Holy Spirit stirs us up, we must come to the same conclusion. We are about to be poured out. We are about to be made a blessing.

Notice the pancake does not pour itself out. That would be a spill, a mess the Maker would have to clean up. No, the pancake mix rests in the container the Maker has provided until the Maker's own hand guides the pouring. We are to act in a similar fashion. We are to be led by the Spirit. We are to be like Jesus when he said: "I tell you the truth, the Son can do nothing by himself; he can do only what he sees his Father doing, because whatever the Father does the Son also does" (John 5:19). This is the nature of being poured out. This is what it means to be a blessing to others.

We live in a nation of those who must "do something" when needs arise or when hungers exist. We must show them how to live a life that is poured out and not become a spill the Maker or someone else has to clean up. The Maker pours out the mix into the hot pan. Oil is poured beforehand to keep the mix from sticking. In the same way, God is at work in every place before us so that we don't get stuck.

When we face the heat, this is our first problem. We're shocked and surprised this is where our Maker has poured us. We want to be formed without getting fried. We want to carry out ministry without opposition. We want everything to change by staying the same. I know it's an insane approach, but it's the one we most often try to take.

Let the pancake teach us the heat is necessary. Without the heat, we would run everywhere. Our ministry would be formless and lack substance. Do not despair. The Maker will turn us when the way is too hot. "Trust in the Lord [Maker] with all your heart. Lean not unto your own understanding. In all your ways acknowledge him and he will direct your paths [movements]" (Proverbs 3:5–6).

Don't flip out when you come in contact with the heat. The Maker has got you in the place that will make you whole. Don't resist his work and end up a "cake not turned" (Hosea 7:8)—a half-baked Christian. You've gone from a mixed up bunch of stuff in a box to finding your place in your Maker's home. You were dry and useless, but the missing ingredient was added to your life. You were stirred up and everything began to come together. Your Maker poured you out, your service only a matter of time.

You faced the heat, and in your Maker's hands you were transformed. Everybody could see the change in you. This is the moment for which you were made. The Maker's spatula slides beneath you. You are lifted up and set down for your Maker's pleasure. You are crowned with sweet syrup. The Parable of the Pancake is coming to its final stage. You are being served.

The Apostle Paul shared this moment with his disciple and son in the faith, Timothy. "For I am now ready to be offered, and the time of my departure is at hand. I have fought a good fight, I have finished [my] course, I have kept the faith. Henceforth there is laid up for me a crown of righteousness, which the Lord, the righteous judge, shall give me at that day: and not to me only, but unto all them also that love his appearing" (2 Timothy 4:4–6).

This is the aim of every disciple: fulfill our course and receive the crowning approval of our Maker. This is what we learn when we understand the Parable of the Pancake!

Now that we understand that we can trust the Maker to transform us, next we will discover how God leads by example in Numbers 6.

The Lord Bless You

In Numbers 6:23–26 the Lord commands Moses to give Aaron and his sons the following instructions to teach the people: "This is how you are to bless the Israelites. Say to them: 'The Lord bless you and keep you; the Lord make his face to shine upon you and be gracious unto you; the Lord turn his face toward you and give you peace.'"

One overriding theme is repeated in this concise outline for blessing. Our steps are to be God-breathed. A sense of intimacy fills this six-fold path. The beginning refrain, "the Lord bless you," invites us to have a constant come to Jesus meeting.

"The Lord bless you" literally reads "the Lord bring you to your knees." We are asked by the blessing to make what is ultimate—"Every knee shall bow and tongue shall confess that Jesus is Lord to the glory of God the Father" (Philippians 2:10–11)—to become immediate and constant.

The Lord begins the blessing with an implied, "Why wait?" Like the Taco Bell® commercial says, waiting is overrated. Now, today, is the best time to accompany God in repentance and to align ourselves with God in submission to God's favor and authority.

If you're going to play, get in the game. Elijah the prophet said to the people, "How long will you waver between two opinions? If the Lord is God, follow him; but if Baal is God, follow him" (1 Kings 18:21). To bless, to be blessed, is a call to worship. That's why we don't do good apart from God's directive. We wouldn't want people to waver between thanking us and thanking God. We want the finale to be played first. "The Lord bless you" is an invitation to others to join us in worshipping God.

... And Keep You

The Lord save you. The Lord garner your trust. The Lord be your shield and defense. "Lions, and tigers, and bears" still threaten us. The scripture says the devil goes about as a lion seeking who he may devour. Leaders promise one thing while they stealthily change their stripes to shift with the latest political wind. Bears tell us in the last few months a third of the country's wealth has evaporated. "Oh, no!" has become "Oh, my!" My pension is down by more than a third. My former representative whom I trusted didn't get reelected. The devil is still devilish.

I want to have someone on my side. I want to know someone has my best interest at heart. Thankfully, I do. The Lord is committed to keeping me within his care: "God is our refuge and strength, an ever-present help in trouble. Therefore we will not fear, though the earth give way and the mountains fall into the heart of the sea, though its waters roar and foam and the mountains quake with their surging" (Psalm 46:1–3).

... Make His Face to Shine Upon You

Nothing is as encouraging as someone who loves you, making his or her face to shine upon you. You know how that feels. The rush of warmth, the wave of joy comes over you when you see that smile. Nothing is impossible to those who know the shine of love's face. Many a young man can get through anything when that shine gets through to him. I could stand up to anything, the toughest curve ball, if Daddy's face shined upon me when I went into the batter's box.

When I see that shine in my wife's eyes, I know I can succeed. I know I can bring us out of the mess in which I've gotten us. That face shining upon me lights my way forward.

The Lord promises us the same light. Paul said it best: "May the Lord Jesus Christ himself, and God our Father, who loved us and by his grace gave us eternal encouragement and good hope, encourage your hearts and strengthen you in every good deed and word" (2 Thessalonians 2:16–17).

... And Be Gracious Unto You

This is important. Some of us feel like no face is shining upon us right now. How are we going to make it? We are going to make it because God asks nothing of us that God doesn't first do himself. When God blessed us—called us to bow the knee—God knew something we tend to forget. God knew he would bow first. God would stoop down, take a piece of clay, and breathe his life into it. That clay would become a living soul.

God would stoop down, take on flesh and blood, and dwell among us. God would be gracious. This is God's modus operandi, his method of operation. Jesus said, "The son of man did not come to be served, but to serve, and give his life as a ransom for many" (Mark 10:45).

In the garden of Gethsemane Jesus prayed for his disciples and exhorted them to pray so they would not fall into temptation. Jesus stooped down, "and being in anguish, he prayed more earnestly, and his sweat was like drops of blood falling to the ground" (Luke 22:44).

This is serious. The Lord being gracious to you is your guarantee against selfishness. The gracious way of the Lord assures us sufficiency. We no longer need to serve, so we can get served. God stoops down, "meets all your need according to his glorious riches in Christ Jesus" (Philippians 4:19), and gives you the call and the power to stoop down and be gracious to others.

... The Lord Turn His Face to You

Paul prays: "I pray that out of his glorious riches, he (the Maker) may strengthen you with power through his Spirit in your inner being" (Ephesians 3:16). We can have the inward confidence to move by faith. We have been reminded God will stoop down. We can run and finish our race even stooping down, even while being gracious. The Lord turns his face toward us.

What does this mean? We can persevere. We can be persistent. Even when we know we might not get it right the first, second, or third time, we will persist. Even if we are in the midst of a downturn, we can stoop down even further and rise equal or as an over comer to the challenges we face.

I think of the Marine Mud Run that is held in Roanoke, Virginia, each year. You run the open trail. You ford the river. You push yourself forward despite the slippery slopes. You can see the finish line. But, you have to crawl through the mud first.

Some pull up short. Some try but pull back. Some slop their way through to the very end. "Oh, how I want to be in that number!" We can be because the Lord turns his face toward us. We may not be able to see it as clearly as we desire, the faces of our enemies and foes looming as large as they do. Rest assured the Lord is there.

It is part of God's favor for you that you don't always see it clearly. God wants the gift of faith to be the deep seeded mark of who you and I are. Writing this book, I have often spent days doing more talking about writing than writing. "I need to finish this chapter. I need to rewrite this section." On and on I would drone about things I needed to do without doing them.

Karen had heard enough. Watching the interview of Chantel Hobbs, author of *Never Say Diet* on the James Robison program, she found her solution. Apparently, Chantel talked incessantly to her husband about needing to write a book about the keys God had taught her in losing 200 pounds. Her husband finally told her, "I don't want to hear anymore."

"Don't talk to me anymore about what you are going to do. Write the book then come and tell me about it." Karen thought this was a great idea.

We made a covenant to do much the same. Karen knows I love to talk. Her refusal to hear anything more about the book that needed to be written is the guarantee she will now get an earful about the book that has been written. What seemed to be a rejection is instead the necessary requirement for accomplishing the goal of finishing *Moving at the Speed of Grace*.

What appeared to be Karen's face turning away from me is the only way I left for her to encourage me forward. Know that God may be blessing you in the same way.

... And Give You Peace

Heaven and earth may pass away but God's covenant of blessing will not. We can strap ourselves in with God. We can move at the speed of grace. Our works, our deeds can match the works of heaven. We are God's ambassadors "as though God were making his appeal through us" (2 Corinthians 5:20). "We implore you on Christ's behalf: be reconciled to God" (2 Corinthians 5:20). Bow the knee. Be blessed.

God stooped down. "God made him who had no sin to be sin for us, so that in him we might become the righteousness of God" (2 Corinthians 5:21). We can make a lasting impression. We can be led by the Holy Spirit. We can be a blessing. We can be in the right place, at the right time, for the right reason, for the right person.

When I first moved into my new church, the days were filled with activity. I had made a commitment to visit the members, and my Day-Timer® was jam packed with appointments and meetings.

One afternoon I got home, and being a little mind numb and weary, I decided to go see a movie. Karen had some things she wanted me to pick up, but they would wait. She told me, "Go, watch the movie first." I got to the theater, plopped down my three dollars for my ticket (a benefit of living in South Hill) and found a good seat. That was easy. There were only a handful of people there. The movie was set for 5:00 p.m. At eight minutes 'til I decided I would quietly pray while I waited. "Get up and leave," were the words that reverberated inside my head. "I just got here," I reasoned. "Get up and leave."

"Lord, I don't know why. I wanted to see the movie. But, Lord, I think this is you."

So, I got up and left. I got my ticket refunded, called Karen on the cell phone, and told her what happened. I told her I might as well run the errands for her. I didn't know if I was missing something, supposed to meet someone or what.

I had moved and gone to the movies. I had received a course correction. Now, I was moving to find some pickling lime and canning salt. Walmart was only a few minutes from the theater so I went there first. They didn't have it.

I drove to Food Lion near our house. They didn't have it. I called Karen back and told her since I didn't know of anything that evening I would just ride until I found the items she wanted. If push came to shove, I could drive to my mama's (an hour away). I knew she had them. Thankfully, I didn't have to go that far. There are two grocery stores in Chase City twenty-one miles up the road. I found one item in one store and the other in the second. Mission accomplished.

As I called Karen back to tell her what time I'd be home for supper, it dawned on me I had promised that Karen and I would attend the Cottage Prayer meeting that evening. With about twenty church members attending, how messed up would I have been if I had missed it at the movies? What a great first impression that would have been! Instead, we had the opportunity to reinforce our previous Sunday's sermon about how God gets into our stuff.

The next night after my last scheduled appointment, I scheduled and went to see the movie. I arrived at the theater this time and had to pay the full four dollar price for the show. But when I walked in, I met the four young men in our church for which I had prayed and asked God, "Could I spend some time with them?"

The answer was standing in front of me. "Yes, you can." We watched the movie together.

SMALL GROUP DISCUSSION QUESTIONS:

1. Discuss the Parable of the Pancake with your group. At what stage is your spiritual life?

2. What are your fears about moving to the next stage of a pancake? In what way does moving forward excite you?

3. What keeps you from receiving the blessing Moses was given for the people?

4. Split into pairs and take turns sharing the blessing with each other. Say it slowly and allow the other person time to receive it.

5. Share with your group about this experience of sharing and receiving the blessing of God from one another.

Bring Life

You are the salt of the earth.

Matthew 5:13

You are the light of the world. A city on a hill cannot be hidden. Neither do people light a lamp and put it under a bowl. Instead they put it on its stand, and it gives light to everyone in the house. In the same way, let your light shine before men, that they may see your good deeds and praise your Father I heaven.

Matthew 5:14–16

Blessed is the influence of one true, loving human soul on another.

—George Eliot

MAKING AN INFLUENTIAL DIFFERENCE

To bring life is to invest yourself in learning how to benefit others from the things that have benefited you. You share out of your passion or pain, and it gives hope and encouragement to others. To bring life you have to give interest and attention to the place where God anoints and brings forth increase in you and for you. Like a good farmer, your work does not end with the harvest. You give interest and attention to the harvest because it is meant for much more than to supply you with ample reserves. The increase God gives you is to serve as resources for others.

Follow the pathway of grace outlined in 1 Corinthians 3, as Paul instructs the church in how God works and gives. He first describes himself and Apollo as "servants through whom you came to believe" (1 Corinthians 3:5). Our role in bringing life is one of cooperating within the goodness of God to bring someone to repentance and faith. Next, Paul describes our part in this process as one of planting, "I planted the seed," and of watering, "Apollo watered it." The harvest is described as the place where God gives us increase or blessing, "But God made it grow" (1 Corinthians 3:6).

It is upon this God-given increase that we bring life. "By the grace God has given me, I laid a foundation as an expert builder, and someone else is building on it … If what he has built survives He will receive his reward" (vv. 10, 14).

I could attribute my lifelong lack of success to skipping over this step of bringing life. I have expected the harvest to insure my breakthrough. It does not. It may have the opposite effect. Let me show you what I mean. The blessing of God in your life is the increase. How you give interest to that increase determines your impact (your ability to bring life) and your eventual breakthrough. Paul had lived out the pathway of grace before the Corinthians and now reminded them of what it looked like.

1. We called you, like God, to begin in repentance so ...
   We were servants through whom you came to believe.

2. We foreknew the need of your heart and ...
   We planted the seed of the Gospel into your life.

3. We knew you were predestined to be conformed into the image of Jesus so ...
   We watered and nurtured your faith.

4. We knew God called you to go beyond yourself and bless others and ...
   We testified that God gave the increase and caused you to grow.

5. We knew God justified you and had you ready to pursue your calling so ...
   We laid the foundation and showed you how to build your life in Jesus.

6. We knew God would be glorified in you. You would pass the tests of life and ...
   We reminded you that you would receive an abundant reward.

Every one of us will be tested. Only the lifeless face no challenges. But I have tried to avoid this section of the road. I've tried to take a shortcut from blessing to breakthrough. I've tried to make my own path. It has just put me in the ditch.

I have been in ministry for over twenty-five years. I serve as a pastor now, but I used to travel as a singer and evangelist. Every place I have gone, God has given people to me—people who would sign up to be on my mailing list. This was my increase: the place of blessing in my life. I tried to make it a place of breakthrough. It didn't work.

It was the point of blessing where I was to serve them, bring life to them, care for them, feed them, and teach them. Instead, I wanted them to feed me. I wanted them to support my ministry. God was supplying seed. I thought he was supplying my need. So, I didn't do anything with the lists.

At this point of inaction I stepped out of grace. I operated under a shadow of debt. I ought to have typed those names into a database. I needed to send out a monthly newsletter. I should learn how to use an autoresponder. I ought to update them on a regular basis. This lack of action created a sense of doubt in the minds of those who did want to bless me. You don't want to support a non-productive entity. I had promised those who signed up that they would be updated and kept informed of future projects and ministry. My lack of fulfillment darkened from a shadow of doubt to a shadow of deceit. As Dr. Edwin Cole used to teach, "A broken promise is a lie."

No wonder I had never prospered in my ministry. If I had operated in grace, each person who ever signed up interested in my ministry would have had their original blessing reinforced and strengthened by what followed. Their faith would have been built up in our message. They would have trusted us and would have told others about us.

But, now I repent. I had believed a lie. What was that lie? I could skip over the movement of God that brings life and still get my breakthrough. I could live off the increase God gave me instead of the interest that was given back to me after I had given interest and care to others.

I cannot think of a single place I have ever been that God hadn't given me at least a 100 percent increase. There's only one of me. I've always had at least one person sign up or give me their contact information. I would not be exaggerating to say there were many places where God gave an increase that was many thousands of a percent.

Instead of giving that increase appreciative care, instead of bringing again the life of God, I let that increase dry up and die. Interested people became names on faded sheets of paper. However, we're changing that. My administrative assistant took that big pile of names and set up a database for me. The Webmaster updated the Web site, and I am now prepared to teach and share the content of what God has been teaching me as this book was written. I'm becoming familiar with Twitter and Facebook. I'm starting to take heed to those whom God has given me oversight. I feed those increased to me.

I live not to be served but to serve. That is where blessing is multiplied and life is brought forth. Dietrich Bonhoeffer wrote, "When Christ calls a man, he bids him come and die" (Cost of Discipleship, 1937). Yes, it is the passionate death of Jesus that brings life to us. It is our passionate death to self that extends that life to others. But, we don't really die. The Apostle Paul said, "I am crucified with Christ; nevertheless I live. Yet, not I, but Christ lives in me and the life that I now live in the flesh I live by faith in the Sin of God" (Galatians 2:20, NKJV).

This step of bringing life must not be missed. This is the step that proves you can get anything you want when you help enough people get what they want. Isaiah prophesied the same outcome for God's work in Jesus Christ. "Therefore I will give him a portion among the great, and he will divide the spoils with the strong, because he poured out his life unto death, and was numbered with the transgressors. For he bore the sin of many, and made intercession for the transgressors" (Isaiah 53:12).

Even though I have been prone to try to skip this step, I know of others who have excelled in bringing life to others. They have utilized their pain, passion, and prayers to profit others more than themselves. I could recount many, but the remainder of this chapter will highlight just a few.

My Parents

I have to begin with my parents. They were as Paul and Apollo were in Corinth. They were the servants through whom I came to believe. They planted the good news of the Gospel into my life from its very beginning, deciding that the first gift I needed on my first Christmas was a Bible. They foreknew that my faith would arise from reading and hearing God's word.

They watered and built up that faith every day. We shared our prayers, conversations, and life together. I was taken to church every Sunday. I was taught how to think and conduct myself as a Christian even before I was one.

Every night I was witness to my daddy getting on his knees beside his bed and praying with God for all of us and for all that concerned us. I remember as a teenager finding a letter he had written to God thanking God for the blessing of seeing all his children come to saving faith.

My parents worked hard so that we could have opportunities they never had. They indeed brought life to us. They lived their whole lives within a three-mile radius of where they were born and raised. Yet, their children and grandchildren have traveled and served in five continents. Some have performed at Disneyworld, on the stage of the Grand Old Opry, and in the Rose Garden at the White House.

Best of all, my parents left us a legacy of knowing how to walk the way of peace. Part of that involves how much our family enjoys each other's company. Another aspect of that way of peace is how much we like to work together. It's actually fun to work. But the greatest way my parents shared the way of peace was how they kept the same peaceful attitude in spite of hardship, adversity, or pain. We once lost a year's income in a twenty-minute tobacco barn fire. I never could tell anything had happened. Even in the last days of battling stomach cancer, my daddy shared the special things God had done for him, like the lightning bug show he got to see when the pain wouldn't allow him to sleep.

As I look back upon it now, the reason we were blessed with such a wonderful life was because my parents brought it to us every day growing up. They walked the pathway of grace. Their lives worked the way God does, and what a difference it has made.

John Eldredge

If you have ever read anything by John Eldredge, you begin to realize that we are called to live an epic life with God. If you have eyes to see, you will notice the whole earth is full of the glory of God. It reflects his handiwork, and we can, too. When I read *The Way of the Wild Heart*, I was struck by how the stages of a man's growth and development into becoming a man of God mirror and reflect the pathway of grace.

One of the reasons I believe that John Eldredge has had such an impact in his ministry is because the way of the wild heart is the way of God's heart. He is describing what it looks like when we are moving at the speed of grace as men. I encourage you to read the books of John Eldredge, especially *The Way of the Wild Heart* now titled *Fathered by God*. Check out his ministry at http://www.ransomedheart.com.

The first stage of a man's development begins as a *son* aligned with his daddy. It is a time of exploration and wonder when any question can be asked, any wild place can be explored, and any feat can be undertaken. This is the time of life when everything is good and when you can be great at everything. This is the season of my life when, at age five, I planted my first garden, learned how to play baseball, and built cities in the plowed ground. At seven I was entrusted with an axe—the handle was broken and it was very dull—to chop down my first tree and begin to build my first fort. That was the year I started digging my first tunnel and when we turned our basement into a bat cave.

The time of being a *son* is when we are to grow "in wisdom and stature and in favor with God and man" (Luke 2:52, KJV). We move like our daddy moves. We stand like our daddy stands. When we grow up, we'll be strong and big like our daddy. In some sense, we will be like Jesus, "always about our Father's business" (Luke 2:49, KJV).

The second stage is that of a *cowboy* or *ranger*. This is when our adventures become real. It's when we enter a wilderness of finding out who we are and what we can really do. Can I trust God the way

Daddy does, or can I trust God in a way that is unique to me? This is a time when you not only want to be like your daddy but you start striving to be as strong as you can be. This is when I started lifting weights. This is when I was a genuine field hand on the farm. This is when I found out I liked to sing and I found out I could learn to do whatever I set my mind to learn.

When I was a cowboy, I learned I could pray about anything, even about who I would someday marry. It's a crazy story but true. I was fourteen. School had just started. It was almost fall, 1974. I had gone out in the backyard to play basketball. It was an unseasonably warm September afternoon, and the thunderclouds were forming in the western sky. I began thinking about a particular girl, Kimberly Ann Tharpe. I had a crush on her and liked her a lot, but she had not returned the favor.

I was shooting along, thinking about our possible future, when I noticed those clouds had gotten a lot closer. In fact, you could see the rain pouring down a couple of miles away. I really wanted to play basketball. I had already included God in my mental discussion on me and Kimberly Ann Tharpe when I decided I would pop the question—to God, that is. I would ask God if she and I were to be married someday, but I didn't want to be too presumptuous. So, I asked God, "If I am to marry a girl whose name starts with K, let the rain stop and let me keep on playing basketball." Well, by then, the rain was only a hundred yards away coming down in sheets over the field. But as I finished my prayer, I felt one big, fat drop hit me square in the forehead and then the line of rain stopped, shifted due south, and I turned around and kept on playing basketball.

Kimberly Ann Tharpe never liked me very much, and that day faded into the memories of my childhood. Fourteen years passed, and someone asked me after I had introduced my wife to them, "Do you spell that with a C or with a K?" When I answered, "You spell Karen with a K," the memory returned.

I had such a memory because I found out as a young cowboy you can trust God for anything under the sky. It was that trust that enabled me to get through the next years of my life.

I entered the third stage, the *warrior*, during high school. Playing football was a part of that. So was being a part of a gospel quartet. Practicing for and competing for a place in the All-Regional and All-State Bands was a way of being a warrior. Running for student government and representing the student body at the school board were part of the mix.

I was asked to lead a group of students in choosing a company to provide our class rings for graduation. We did our research and picked the company that gave us the best price with the most options. But, when I reported our choice, I found out the school administrator had already chosen another company. I had to apologize to our group for wasting their time. I had to apologize to the company we had chosen for the promise we broke. The warrior in me took responsibility and then protested the whole process by refusing as class president to purchase a class ring. The stage of the warrior is where we battle for strength and confidence. Again, I have to give thanks for the way I had seen my daddy pray, read the Bible, and find strength for the decisions he had to make through them. When I left home for college, I had to learn how to enter that warrior phase in a different way.

The opening week of orientation, a girl involved with campus ministry met me in the middle of the campus and asked me a question: "Are you a fundamentalist?" I grew up near Lynchburg, Virginia, so I would get that question a lot. But this was the first time. I thought, *Fundamental means basic, and I believe the basic things,* so I replied, "Yeah, I guess so." She walked off and didn't speak to me for several weeks.

I was a religion and English major, and I had one professor who divided each small class in a unique way. He would classify us and seat us accordingly around the common table we shared. The "fundies" sat on one side of the table, the liberals on the other side. The moderates he would place at the end of the table, and he wouldn't allow them to speak. The professor asserted they didn't have an opinion anyway, so they would not be allowed to speak in class. It made for an interesting learning environment, where the professor seemed to make questioning and sifting our faith his personal challenge. The good news is that I took as much pleasure in answering and justifying my faith as he did in calling it into question. By the time I went to seminary, all the gauntlets had already been thrown down.

This did not relieve me of developing as a warrior. As one visiting preacher so aptly pointed out one day in chapel, we who had been accepted into seminary because of the outward demonstration of our call must battle to overcome the practice of hiding and privatizing our sins. One of those battles was long and ongoing as I entered more deeply into the next phase of the *lover*.

Eldredge writes that the lover stage is to captivate our heart not only for the sake of the opposite sex but even more for the sake of obedient service. This stage is not only to be marked by the lust of the eye or the lust of the flesh but even more by the appreciation for what is good and beautiful. The strength of the lover is that he can see and find joy in what is unseen. This begins with the heart of God and also finds joy in the heart of friends, male or female.

It is the stage of the lover that best expresses the demeanor of one who is called to be a blessing. Just as Jesus was moved with compassion when he looked upon people, there is a romance to grace that moves us as well.

I am blessed to have loved and been married to Karen Elizabeth Ramsey for over twenty-one years. She has helped me appreciate many things to which I would have remained blind without her in my life. I still have eyes though. I still notice what is comely and attractive. I remember my first trip to Brazil. The churches where we ministered were filled with beautiful Brazilian women. I reminded myself that I was a married man, but it was a gracious word from God that set me free to love and bless each one of them. God whispered, "You didn't know you had so many beautiful sisters, did you?" I had to laugh and admit I hadn't realized until then where the looks went in the family.

God is getting us up to speed, moving us in rhythm with his grace. God wants to entrust more and more responsibility to us.

The heart of God wants to safely trust you and me as we find our safety and trust in him.

Whoever God calls, he justifies. God wants to know we are good to go because God is moving us into the next phase: that of the *king*. The king is entrusted by God to "wield power, influence, and property in his name." (Eldredge, 2006, 219–220) Proverbs 21:1 says, "The king's heart is in the hand of the Lord, like the rivers of water, He turns it wherever He wishes" (NKJV). This is the anointing of a king: to reach the heart of any matter, to cut like water down to the bedrock of any problem or situation. You are so moved by the Spirit of God that whatever you touch is touched by God.

This is a lifelong prayer of mine and I hope yours, too. *Lord, enable me to become a habitat, a walking ecosystem of grace and revival. Give me wisdom to care for those you've entrusted to my care. Let my love make a difference. Let me share the testimony of those saints who walking into a town or place were accompanied by the conviction of your Holy Spirit. Above all, let me not desire the credit for any good thing, but always give you praise and honor. Let me be as a servant who has the good sense to know any good thing I do is what I was supposed to be doing anyway.*

The last stage of manhood is that of the *sage*. Their experience of life is only overmatched by their experience of grace. They don't let their knowledge get ahead of their understanding. They can accomplish what is necessary without the necessity of pride. Therefore, they are seeking those with whom they can share their wisdom. They are happy to share what they know and happy not to share if no one is ready to listen.

Sages have come full circle. They understand like any good son, as John Wesley said shortly before he died, "the best thing of all is that God ("Abba"—Daddy) is with us." They know, like the cowboy, that the biggest adventure is still ahead. Like the warrior, they have fought a good fight, and they have kept the faith. Their reward is ready. The lover in the sage is stirred up, for soon their heart's desire will be fulfilled and what they've only seen in part they will embrace face to face. Like the King, they just want to hear, "Well done, good and faithful servant; you have been faithful over a few things, I will make you a ruler over many things. Enter into the joy of your Lord" (Matthew 25:23, NKJV).

Dave Ramsey

Syndicated radio host, *Fox Business News* personality, and *New York Times* bestselling author, Dave Ramsey, shares his past pain and present passion to bring people to a place of Financial Peace (www.daveramsey.com). Almost every day, Dave invites you to a place where "Debt is dumb, cash is king, and the paid off home mortgage has taken the place of the BMW as the status symbol of choice" (The Dave Ramsey Show, syndicated radio and Fox Business News host).

I first heard Dave Ramsey on a local radio station in Nashville, Tennessee. Later, I appreciated his ministry more when we began a Financial Peace University class (www.daveramsey.com/fpu/home) at our church. It was there I was introduced to Dave's Baby Steps to Financial Peace. They are as follows:

Step 1: $1,000 in an Emergency Fund

Step 2: Pay Off All Debt with the Debt Snowball

Step 3: 3 to 6 Months Expenses in Savings

Step 4: Invest 15 percent of Income into Roth IRA's and Pre-tax Retirement Plans

Step 5: College Funding

Step 6: Pay Off Your Home Early

Step 7: Build Wealth and Give!

Why do I think these steps are so helpful in bringing life to people? Number one, they are concrete and incremental. They are specific. They are measurable. They are attainable. They are relevant to the situation in which people find themselves. Followed over time, the difference they can make is unavoidable.

The difference is unavoidable because the Baby Steps are framed on the pathway of God's grace. If you would be faithful in following these steps, soon you will be moving at the speed of grace. Dave suggests these steps are just common sense financial responses, and he's right. However, it is amazing how much godly wisdom looks like common sense when it's used. Proverbs 22:3 says, "The prudent man foresees [the] evil and hides himself, but the simple pass on and are punished" (NKJV).

Dave Ramsey has brought life to many by being concerned about those who are paying "stupid tax," suffering and being punished for their lack of financial wisdom. I say wisdom on purpose. Wisdom is knowledge applied appropriately. Sharing these baby steps has given many a set of behaviors that enabled their knowledge to be applied appropriately. But, let's look at the Baby Steps and how they correspond to the way God works. An emergency fund, $1,000 in the bank is the first baby step. You must be prepared for reality. Every circumstance must not find you lost in the red, paying needless penalties, fees, and interest.

Just as God calls you to repentance, Dave Ramsey insists you need to bring your life into proper alignment with reality. Know what you are doing. The beginning of the journey is not a mystery. Our activity needs to change. Our budget replaces our best guess and we begin to save.

The second baby step is to initiate the debt snowball. Tackling our debts from the least to the greatest with "cheetah-like" intensity is a visible exchange of our old ways for what is new. By focusing our faith, a course to freedom is opened. Dave Ramsey repeats, "If you will live like no one else, later you can live like no one else" (2003, 1).

The third step, three to six months of expenses, reflects the realization and the determination we are going to operate from a position of strength. It is the only way we can move into being able to bless other people.

I put the fourth and fifth baby steps together. We are going to be blessed and extend that blessing to our children. We will prepare for the future. We will not become a burden to society or the responsibility of others. We will take responsibility for ourselves and bless others by the simple fact that they will be free to pursue the calling of God upon their lives without paying for ours.

Paying off our home early, the sixth step, frees us to impact the lives of others in a powerful way. What would you be at liberty to do if you had no obligations above your living expenses? You would be free to serve and not have to ask for anything in return.

The last baby step, building wealth and giving, is your launching pad for breakthrough. You laid the foundation for that breakthrough when you built a fund for facing emergencies. Now you are investing and saving for emergent opportunities.

Building wealth makes you the wise farmer that saves seed for the greater harvests the future will bring. This is as Dave Ramsey describes financial peace! God says something needs to be done. No problem! I'm not a financial baby anymore. I am a coworker with God. I am calling others to walk the walk as I did. Dave Ramsey reminds us of that almost every time he closes out his syndicated radio show: "There's ultimately only one way to financial peace and that's to walk daily with the Prince of Peace, Christ Jesus!"

SMALL GROUP DISCUSSION QUESTIONS:

1. What blessings has God brought to you in your spiritual journey?

2. How can your blessings be used to encourage someone else in their spiritual journey?

3. Which stage of the spiritual life (as per Eldredge) would describe your spiritual life at this time? (*Son, Cowboy, Warrior, Lover, King, or Sage.*)

4. How could you progress in these stages?

5. What might need to be done with your finances in order to allow you to be more available to serve others?

MAKING PASSIONATE PROGRESS

Bringing life is taking blessing to the next level. Jesus blessed people in his ministry, but his ministry had a goal beyond that. Jesus said, "The Son of Man has come to seek and to save that which was lost" (Luke 19:10, NKJV). How was he going to do that? He chose disciples. He taught and healed. But the pivotal event, the fulcrum upon which his greatest influence was exerted, was the cross. This is the embodiment of Jesus' passion.

Bringing life begins with the coordination of vision and action. Jesus' vision to seek and save coordinated his action in the cross. This coordination of vision and action had long been prophesied. Read Psalm 22. The crucifixion of Jesus is the sacrificial gift of God that causes "The ends of the earth to remember and turn to the Lord" (Psalm 22:27). Read Isaiah 53. Jesus is exalted as Lord because "He poured out his life unto death, and was numbered with the transgressors. For he bore the sin of many, and made intercession for the transgressors" (Isaiah 53:12).

Jesus' passion sets the example for us. His precious blood sows the seed of life for us. Get a clear picture of the cross. See what Jesus is willing to suffer for your sake. Hear his words. Experience his agony. They are our birth pangs.

Jesus died on the cross to bring life. "For Christ died for sins once for all, the righteous for the unrighteous, to bring you to God" (1 Peter 3:18). Jesus said, "But I, when I am lifted up from the earth, will draw all men to myself" (John 12:32). According to John, Jesus said this to show how he would die.

When you bring life to someone, you coordinate vision and action. Your pain or passion is offered to profit others. You tell your story. Others identify with it. There is coordination of vision as others find themselves in your experience.

Your life is a unique story. It is also a unique solution. Grace has brought you safe thus far. Inquiring minds want to know how it was done. Wounded hearts want to know how you were brought back to life. Weary souls want to know how you got your second wind. How did you make it? We need to show others that they can make it. When I was a young boy, I heard this joke· Why did the chicken cross the road? The answer: To get to the other side. Later, the question was asked again. Why did the chicken cross the road? The answer is to show the opossum it could be done.

Every day people are killing themselves trying to find their way through life. Some are killing others as well as themselves. Violence is the natural solution into which sin slides. Something has to give. John 3:16 tells us that God gave. The passion of the cross says Jesus gives. When we bring life, we choose to give.

How do we find the resources and strength to do this? We access grace. We act in the authority of God's indwelling Holy Spirit. When something has to give, we share what we have received bringing life in Jesus' name.

To bring life, we have to coordinate vision and action. Read Acts 10 where the good news that brings life is expanded to include the Gentiles. Cornelius, a God-fearing member of the Italian Regiment received an angelic vision in answer to his prayers. Cornelius received this command.

> Now send men to Joppa to bring back a man named Simon, who is called Peter. He is staying with Simon the tanner, whose house is by the sea. When the angel who spoke to him had gone, Cornelius called two of his servants and a devout soldier who was one of his attendants. He told them everything that had happened and sent them to Joppa.
>
> Acts 10:5–8

A new life is definitely on the way for Cornelius for he has coordinated vision and action. As these three men are finding their way to the Apostle Peter, God continues to move.

The Apostle Peter is given a vision from God. Three times Peter's view of things is challenged. Three times God instructs Peter, "Do not call anything impure what God has made clean" (Acts 11:9). As Peter tries to figure out what this means, three men show up at his door asking for him. Without vision we would never move beyond our comfort zones. We would never rise above our upbringing or reach beyond our present abilities. We would cease to grow.

Peter had gone up on the roof of the house to pray when the vision came. Clarity was given to Peter through the arrival of the three men. Peter coordinated his actions in alignment with the vision, and when he did, life sprang forth. Before he could even finish his sermon to those in Cornelius' house, the Holy Spirit came on all those who heard his message.

The Apostle Paul also demonstrates to us that bringing life is taking blessing to the next level, coordinating vision and action. Paul had a traumatic conversion experience. It left him blind and unable to eat or drink anything for three days. A vision came to Paul as he was praying, revealing his call and disclosing the fact that a man named Ananias would come, lay hands on him, and he would recover his sight.

It is the call of God that reveals and fleshes out God's vision for this newly formed apostle. We have the description of that call as the Lord commands Ananias, "Go! This man is my chosen instrument to carry my name before the Gentiles and their kings and before the people of Israel. I will show him how much he must suffer for my name" (Acts 9:15).

Follow Paul from that point forward. For fourteen years Paul puts first what God had put second: "Carry my name before the people of Israel" (Acts 9:15). For fourteen years, Paul moves in blessing responsive to God's call. But, watch how in Acts 19, when Paul coordinates his actions with the primary aspect of God's vision: "To carry my name before the Gentiles," Paul's ministry explodes in its influence.

> Paul entered the synagogue and spoke boldly there for three months, arguing persuasively about the kingdom of God. But some of them became obstinate; they refused to believe and publicly maligned the Way. So Paul left them. He took the disciples with him and had discussions daily in the lecture hall of Tyrannus. This went on for two years, so that *all the Jews and Greeks who lived in the province of Asia heard the word of the Lord.* God did extraordinary miracles through Paul, so that even handkerchiefs and aprons that had touched him were taken to the sick, and their illnesses were cured and the evil spirits left them
>
> Acts 19:8–12

To bring life is to coordinate vision and action. Ask any couple who wants to have a family, "What will you do to make it happen?" They will answer in one form or another, "Coordinate vision and action."

This brings us to another ingredient in bringing life. The action we take is concentrated or focused in specific activity, with specific people, and in a specific time. Jesus' coordination of vision and action led him to "resolutely set out for Jerusalem" (Luke 9:51). We see his concentration in the Upper Room as Jesus breaks the bread and shares the cup with his disciples. We see this concentration in the garden of Gethsemane as Jesus "prayed more earnestly, and his sweat was like drops of blood falling to the ground" (Luke 22:44). We see Jesus enduring the mocking and beating and scourging. We see him wear the crown of thorns and bear the cross.

You hear the heartbeat of that concentration as he speaks on behalf of his executioners, "Father, forgive them; for they do not know what they are doing" (Luke 23:34). You hear it as he tells the thief on the adjacent cross, "I tell you the truth, today, you will be with me in Paradise" (Luke 23:43). You sense his final breath concentrates his vision of bringing life down to one sentence. "Father, into Your hands I commit My spirit" (Luke 23:46, NKJV).

Bringing life is the coordination of vision and action. It is the concentration of that action in a specific way. For Peter, it was concentrated on Cornelius and his household. For Paul, it was concentrated in the hall of Tyrannus. These are not the only times they brought life to others, but they serve as illustrations for us.

What about the rest of us? Where do we concentrate our activity? If you have a business, how do you market to your customers? If you lead a team, how do you position and train your players to perform their best? If you're a parent, how do you demonstrate love to your children and awaken the vision of life God has for them?

Karen and I shared a vision of having a family. We coordinated that vision with suitable actions, yet we were still unable to have children. We decided a different track was in order and took training to become foster parents. A few months after finishing our training, we received a call. There were two small children in need of a home. Could we take one of them? We said, "Yes" and concentrated our love on twenty-two-month old Cody.

We picked him up from Vanderbilt hospital. He was in a body cast and riding in a little red wagon when we loaded him in our car and took him home. I can't tell the whole story in these pages, but we concentrated our love to bring him life. We taught him to walk again after the cast was removed. We capped his teeth that had almost rotted away. What a grill he had! We expanded his vocabulary from the four words he knew when he came to us. We taught him how to trust us and not be afraid.

It wasn't easy. We received another call a little more than two months later. Could we keep two more children for two weeks? I thought we could do anything for two weeks, so we again said yes and the process of concentrating our efforts began again.

It got harder. The problem in the former foster home did not go away in two weeks. We began to find out through sleepless nights and trials by fire what had happened. Karen had to be put into the hospital from dehydration and exhaustion. I was under suspicion of abusing the children because things came to light under our care. Again the whole story can't be told here, but we persevered.

Seven months after Cody came to us they called and then came and got him. He went back to his grandmother. That lasted two months until his grandfather called one night around 11:00 p.m. and said, "Come get him."

We could hear him crying inside the house when we got out of our car in the driveway. When we walked in the door, his crying stopped. He walked over to me. I picked him up. He laid his head down on my shoulder and went to sleep. We took him back home with us that night.

A year passed, and they came for him again. This time he would be given back to his mother. That lasted nine months before they hurt him again. Once more, we received a call. This time the call came from his mother, but let me stop and share what happened right before we got that call.

Karen and I were coming back home from Knoxville driving west on I-40. We were talking when Karen shared something that had happened the week before. She narrated to me that she had been having dreams of Cody, bad dreams, and had contacted Cody's grandmother to see how he was doing. Through the grandmother, Karen got the mother's phone number and had talked to her.

I wanted to know every word of their conversation and pestered Karen to tell me. She said, "This is why I didn't tell you last week. I knew you would be this way." She proceeded to tell me how rough it was and that she was concerned for Cody's safety. But, she was glad she had called. I was too. When we got home, there was a message on the machine from Cody's mother letting us know Cody had been hurt and was back in Vanderbilt hospital.

Thank God for the dreams Karen had. Thank God she coordinated her actions in alignment with them. Thank God she concentrated those actions in calling the grandmother and then the mother. A week or so later, Cody was back home with us, this time for good.

During the time Cody had been gone, we received two more calls. The first was from the doctor telling us we wouldn't be able to have any children of our own. We cried. We held on to each other, and we cried some more. Then the other call came. Could we keep a little nine-day old baby girl named Hannah? We said, "Yes."

Do you know what the name Hannah means? It means favored. The first call I thought meant we were no longer favored by God. The second call revived my hope that we were.

With Hannah, like Cody, like Jamie and James, and many other children we have had in our home, we began to concentrate our love to bring them life. Eventually, this concentrated action led us to adopt the four children who had stayed in our home. I am now the proud daddy of four: Sandra Michelle, James Keith, Robert Cody, and Hannah Elizabeth.

This brings us to see the last aspect of bringing life. We are consistent over time. We coordinate vision and action. We concentrate our actions on a specific person or need and in a specific place or time. Doing this with consistency over time will bring life.

This is how it works in bringing life naturally or spiritually. A vision or desire is shared. A couple comes together in an act of love. By faith, the sperm and the egg produce the seed of a living soul. That seed is nurtured in the womb until that baby is born. The process, though, is not complete. We expect that baby to grow and mature and eventually get together with someone in love and repeat the process themselves.

Life is meant to be full. Jesus said, "I have come that they may have life and have it to the full" (John 10:10). We are consistent over time to insure that life is brought to fullness. We call it a tragedy or a miscarriage if that doesn't happen.

We are meant to do well. We were meant to prosper. We were designed by God for improvement, for sanctification. We are called to pursue the fullness of God's Holy Spirit. We are to pursue a full and fulfilling life. We are called to pursue the ways we can bring that fullness of life to others. We are to "make every effort to live in peace with all men and to be holy; without holiness no one will see the Lord" (Hebrews 12:14).

How do we do that? We mimic God. We see the way God works. We move at the speed of grace. We notice how God coordinates vision and action. We study to know and communicate how God concentrates his mercy and displays his justice. We observe how God, consistent over time, calls people, nations, and the whole earth to pursue or follow God.

The Apostle Paul instructs Timothy in this pursuit. "But you, man of God... pursue righteousness, godliness, faith, love, patience, and meekness" (1 Timothy 6:11). The word *pursue* means we are becoming a "dread attendant" of the Lord. Let's change our name to Igor to get a sense of what this pursuit means. "Yes, Master," are our two favorite words. We are beginning to anticipate our Master's wishes.

In the cartoons with which I grew up, the heroes had sidekicks; only villains had attendants. They were to know what their master wanted before he wanted it. I apologize, but when I picture this in my mind, I see Marty Feldman as he appeared in the movie *Young Frankenstein!*

As you live a life of breakthrough moving at the speed of grace, this will more and more describe you. You will anticipate and attend to what your master prefers. If you've been married a long time or in any relationship for a long time, you learn the way the other person likes things. Recently, when Karen was in the hospital, I could help her get comfortable more quickly than the nurses could because I've been with her longer. Walking with God works the same way.

You can do anything. Nothing is impossible to you when you become the "dread attendant" of the Lord. You don't know any better. The Master speaks, and you assume it can be done.

I learned this lesson from my daddy. We used to have target practice in the backyard. My brother, Dennis, Daddy, and I took turns shooting cans off the fence post with the twenty-two-rifle. I remember the day when I took my turn and Daddy noticed I was blinking when the gun fired. He wanted to break me of this. Blinking threw my shot off an inch or two and caused me to miss seeing what I shot. Daddy first asked me to stop. He wanted me to follow the bullet and tell him where it hit the can. I still blinked.

Daddy's next solution was to give Dennis his turn. Daddy then set me off to the side, so I could see Dennis and the target at the same time. Daddy said I was far enough away from the firing of the gun to keep from blinking. So, when Dennis shot, I was to follow his bullet and tell him where it hit the can.

I did.

I know what you're thinking, "You can't do that." Yes, you can. If Daddy said it could be done, then I could do it. Now, Jesus is greater than my daddy. Jesus is faithful and true. "Give thanks to the Lord for he is good. His love endures forever" (Psalm 136:1). Jesus is himself—the same yesterday, today, and forever. Now, if Jesus says it, you can do it. You are his "dread attendant."

Keep on keeping on. You are no longer slow as sin. You are moving at the speed of grace. This has been our goal all along. This is the root of breakthrough. We believe our greatest success is realizing what we and God can do together.

Some say I'm a peculiar person. I like things a certain way. I like a peanut butter sandwich with the peanut butter spread smoothly and exactly on a single slice of bread, then folded into a triangular shape like a handkerchief is folded.

My wife would never fix a peanut butter sandwich for me any other way. She also knows I don't like sweets. So, on my birthday my candles are set, not on a cake, but on a biscuit or on top of a chicken pot pie. For me that's just the right way to do it.

We have seen God has a way he does things. Jesus fulfilled it, and now we are called to follow or attend to this way. That is why Paul tells Timothy, as a man of God, to attend to this righteousness. Attend to this right way of doing things.

Align yourself with the will and pleasure of your Lord. Do things the way the Lord does. This is your reasonable worship. This is how you pursue godliness. In our house, this is why we have two kinds of spaghetti whenever we eat spaghetti. There is Mama's spaghetti and Daddy's spaghetti. I love Mama (Karen, my wife). She loves me. We want each other to fully enjoy the spaghetti experience. So, we make a version of what each of us likes best. Attending to godliness means we actively pursue worship that is good for God and us. One size, one style doesn't fit all.

There was an older gentleman who came to church even though he was blind and couldn't hear well. Someone asked him, "Why do you come to church?" He replied, "I just want to let folks know on whose side I am." Attending to godliness means we are actively exercising our faith in a way that shows whose side we're on.

Writing this book is such an exercise. Caring for my wife when she recovered from surgery was, too. Calling on others for help would be such an exercise for me. What would it be for you? How will you attend to godliness? How will you exercise your faith and show you are on the Lord's side?

Paul tells Timothy he can do that by building up his faith and multiplying the credibility of the gospel by adding his own. Attend to faith. Practice what you preach, so you can preach what you practice. Attend to faith; show others what is possible when God is at work in your life.

Attend to love. Breakthroughs are never meant to be exclusive and personal. Imagine a medical breakthrough that doesn't help patients. That is a contradiction. Breakthroughs are meant to be shared. Breakthroughs without love lead to destruction. Breakthroughs with love bring life.

We were meant to bring life. We were meant for breakthroughs. Don't let anyone tell you we are not. Attend to love so that others who fear the changed life that breakthroughs bring may set their fears aside.

Attend to love so that breakthroughs can be good things. A fellow once asked my daddy, "Don't you want to farm like the Amish did? Daddy hastily replied, "No, I've worked all my life so I wouldn't have to farm like the Amish." Daddy worked to take advantage of breakthroughs.

I bet my Mama would say a washer and dryer work better than hand washing, hand wringing, and hand drying clothes. Even the Amish use machines to milk their cows.

I believe the most shocked reaction I ever saw in my children was when I asked them one time to forgo the breakthrough of toilet tissue for leaves. They insisted if I loved them, I would take them home to go to the bathroom.

Breakthroughs also require testing. This is why Paul again tells Timothy, "Pursue patience" (1 Timothy 6:11). Patience is defined as cheerful or hopeful endurance. Without patience, breakthroughs may fall short of their intended promise. They may not receive the encouragement and correction and/or refinement they need.

I play guitar. It is of great help in my ministry. There are services I could not conduct without it. But I can remember the first time I tried to play the guitar. I was a youth director. After my youth group heard my first attempt at guitar playing, they begged me to stop. They said, "Norm, if you want to love people, if you want to act as a Christian, never try that again." And, I didn't for a long time.

Five years later, I got married. Karen knew how much I loved music and bought me a beautiful guitar. I didn't pick it up. Ten years went by. I was acting as music director for a three-day spiritual experience called The Walk to Emmaus. Others were playing. I was directing. We were asked to play some old hymns with which no musician was familiar. I told them I had a guitar at home. I would locate the chords, and they could play the songs. It probably took me ten or fifteen minutes to find the right spot for my fingers. But by the time I had the chords written out for the other musicians, I felt brave enough to try to play at one of my churches the week before The Walk. It was a disaster. The silver lining? I thought I had found a new weight loss plan because I was sweating profusely when I tried to play the two-chord hymn, "*Nothing But the Blood.*" But God had patience even if I or no one else did. The opening of the event arrived, and the lead guitarist for the weekend didn't show up. That was Thursday night. By Sunday afternoon, my guitar playing wasn't so bad.

Attend to patience. Paul says that's the only way love will come to its desired goal!

Finally, Paul directs Timothy to attend to meekness. No matter what has happened up until now, God wants you moving forward together with him. You can be flexible. Like Muhammad Ali, "You float like a butterfly and sting like a bee." "Shrewd as snakes and as innocent as doves" (Matthew 10:16)—that's you.

"Fight the good fight of faith. Take hold of the eternal life to which you were called when you made your good confession in the presence of many witnesses. In the sight of God, who gives life to everything, and of Christ Jesus, who while testifying before Pontius Pilate made the good confession, I charge you to keep this command without spot or blame until the appearing of our Lord Jesus Christ" (1 Timothy 6:12–14).

Attend to the way of God. Keep moving at the speed of grace.

SMALL GROUP DISCUSSION QUESTIONS:

1. What is your vision for your spiritual life?

2. What do you think God has ahead on your journey with Him?

3. How might your vision need to change to match God's vision for you?

4. What needs to be more consistent about your time with God and your spiritual growth?

5. What is the first aspect of your spiritual life that needs attention? How will your attending to it help others know a better spiritual life?

Breakthrough

Those he justified; he also glorified.

Romans 8:30

We know that anyone born of God does not continue in sin; the one who was born of God keeps himself safe, and the evil one cannot harm him. We know that we are children of God and that the whole world is under the control of the evil one. We know also that the Son of God has come and has given us understanding, so that we may know him who is true—even in his Son Jesus Christ. He is the true God and eternal life.

1 John 5:18–20

Have courage for the great sorrows of life and patience for the small ones; and when you have laboriously accomplished your daily task, go to sleep in peace. God is awake.

—Victor Hugo

MAPS FOR OUR JOURNEY

To attend to the way of God, you need a course of action. You need clues to recognize where you are and where you need to go. I trust you can now recite by heart how God moves in our lives. Follow the way. Let it be your spiritual road map.

I trust you know God begins everything he does with a call to repentance—a call to align our way with God's. The Apostle Paul goes so far to say that all of God's goodness is to bring you and me to alignment and accompaniment with God (Romans 2:4). This alignment or agreement between us and God is not forced. It is God's pleasure to trust us to trust him. We believe, and everything begins to change. We build up that relationship of faith by praying—opening lines of communication powered by the Holy Spirit. Moved by the Spirit, we bless others. We impact them, bringing life in Jesus' name.

What remains? We begin to establish this path of life as our own. This is a life of breakthrough. Don't think it's something unfamiliar. Our lives are filled with breakthroughs.

If you've read this book through to this page, you had to have experienced a breakthrough in your life somewhere in the past. One of the memorable examples of breakthrough in my life was the SRA Reading Program at Phenix Elementary School in Phenix, Virginia. I moved with others from color to color and level to level. The joy of accomplishment, winning over yourself and your past performance, is part and parcel of living a life of breakthrough.

We've all broken through from one grade level to another. We moved from elementary school to middle school and from middle school to high school. We experienced a breakthrough when we graduated from high school or earned our G. E. D.

When we got our driver's license, we experienced a breakthrough. When we moved from home and made it on our own, we experienced a breakthrough. All of us have accomplishments. We all have milestones we have reached. What are yours?

Breakthrough is progress. Breakthrough is acceleration into a new level of efficiency. Breakthrough is awareness that becomes comprehension. You understand how to move forward. You can even draw others forward.

I remember the first time Daddy took me to the field with him to pick corn. He showed me how it was supposed to be done. He assigned me a row, and we started our work. I was so slow. The tractor edged the wagon forward, and we were to pick and pitch our way down the row. I constantly had to yell for the tractor to stop, so I could catch up. Meanwhile, Daddy was up ahead finishing his section and crossing over to help me.

The next year was a breakthrough year. I was now familiar with how to coordinate what I was asked to do and what I could actually do. I kept up with the tractor just fine.

You've heard this process described before. An artist has a breakout single. An athlete has a breakout season. They have practiced themselves into a new level of performance. What about you? Can you accelerate into a new level of faithfulness or reliability? Yes, you can!

You can be an expert or a model others consult. You could be a little league baseball coach or a recreation league basketball coach. You could be a scout leader. You could be the mom who the children of the neighborhood come to for cookies or counsel. You could be the teacher that inspires your students and colleagues.

You could be the business person whom others respect, after whom others want to model their success. You could be the wife who respects and trusts her husband. You could be a husband who loves his wife and gives himself for her.

You become an accomplished practitioner, person, and Christian. I know someone who is accomplished as a praying person. I've heard people say when they are in great need, "I need a 'Jean' prayer." Jean is a wonderful Christian lady. She has practiced and developed her prayer life for most of her eighty-plus years. But you don't have to practice that long to be effective.

When our daughter Hannah was a few years old, she went with me to visit someone in the hospital. There, she prayed for the patient who had a miraculous turn around later that day. After that, everyone wanted me to bring Hannah if I was coming to visit.

When Hannah was five or six years old, we noticed her exhibiting an allergic reaction to something. She would break out in a rash or have hives, and we finally figured out she was allergic to chocolate. That's a terrible thing to find out, especially right before Halloween. We, of course, made the rule she could not eat chocolate anymore. After Trick-or-Treating, she had to trade away all of her chocolate candy to her brothers and sister. She didn't like it one bit.

The next morning, Karen and I were in the kitchen when Hannah walked in and asked for chocolate. I told her she couldn't have any chocolate because it made her break out. She said, "Daddy, Jesus told me I wasn't allergic to chocolate anymore. I could have all I want." I told her what the doctor had told us, and again she said, "But, Jesus told me I'm not allergic anymore."

We gave her chocolate. She is still eating it.

Many of you, I'm sure, would love a chocolate breakthrough. The truth be told, Hannah's breakthrough was not about chocolate. It was about faith. It was about believing what Jesus said. All of our breakthroughs arise from the same tomb—the tomb of our doubts and unbelief. The hardness of our heart must be rolled away so the sun of righteousness can shine! Believing the least about ourselves has to give way to the accomplishments of God's Holy Spirit at work in our lives.

We're pressing forward toward the goal for which we were created. We're pressing in to walk in unity and harmony with God. We're skipping along the road hand-in-hand with our maker and friend. From the very beginning, God called us to follow after him. God foreknew the best route we could follow would be the way of believing in him. By faith, we were predestined to be built up in our faith, conformed into the image of Jesus.

God continues his work and calls us to represent his kingdom and his righteousness. We are ambassadors of blessing. We bring the redemptive life of God to those who are lost and undone. God justifies us, and we are good to go.

We do not try to skate over problems. We immediately ask God to show us what is the heart or root of a matter. We want to know: *how is God going to make all things new today?* We also want to know, *If I can learn something new every day, what is it I need to learn today that will enable me to tag along with God?*

We can live a life of breakthrough. Whoever God justifies, God glorifies. What does it mean to be glorified by God? It means God will finish what he starts in us. It is a great promise of God and one of my favorites. 1 Thessalonians 5:23–24 says:

> May God himself, the God of peace, sanctify you through and through. May your whole spirit, soul, and body be kept blameless at the coming of our Lord Jesus Christ. The one who calls you is faithful, and he will do it.

Notice that last phrase—"he will do it." Jesus will glorify us. He will be faithful to keep the connection of peace secure. He will be faithful to give us the very Spirit of Holiness. Jesus will be faithful to bring us to a place of fitness and wholeness in our spirit, soul, and body.

God is not doing a partial or compartmentalized work in us. God is strengthening our hearts, renewing our minds, restoring our souls, and quickening our mortal bodies.

The Apostle Paul says no amount of discipline or hardship or suffering is to be compared to the glory that will be revealed in us. Stop and consider what I'm saying. Do not discount or delay to some pie-in-the-sky moment the work of God in your life. So often, God's work lacks profundity in us because we believe and expect so little.

Think about it. Whet your lips. Whet your mind and heart, and ask God to reveal his glory.

Turn to the book of Acts. Read through it. It's only about twenty-five pages. See how many times God's glory breaks through. Note how many times the presence of God by the Holy Spirit is revealed. Follow the lives of Peter and John, Stephen, Saul-turned-Paul, Cornelius, and other ordinary Christians through which God did extraordinary things.

The Apostle Paul says these extraordinary events were played out in response to a vision (Acts 26:19). God was moving on purpose through ordinary people so that the glory of God was made plain to the eyes of men. The Lord Jesus told Paul this was his goal for both the Jews and Gentiles. "I am sending you to them to open their eyes and turn them from darkness to light and from the power of Satan to God, so that they may receive forgiveness of sins and a place among those who are sanctified by faith in me" (Acts 26:17–18).

These and all the mighty acts that are recorded in the book of Acts rest on two undeniable facts: the resurrection of Jesus and the reality of the Holy Spirit who comes to reside in the heart and mind of all those who repent and believe.

I simply say to you, God has not changed since those days. Whoever God calls, God justifies. And whoever God justifies, God glorifies. Even as Jesus' death frees us, his resurrection empowers us to live a life of breakthrough!

One of the enemies of living a life of breakthrough is living the life we're used to. We can see this illustrated in the Old Testament, modeled by the nation of Israel. The people seemed locked in a never ending cycle of God saving them; they give thanks for their deliverance, backslide back into sin, and have to be rescued all over again. The habits of their lives are interrupted by God's intervention but never essentially changed. (Deliverance → Backsliding → Renewal.)

The pathway of grace provides us a different path to follow. In Christ, God is saving us, we are giving thanks and praise for our deliverance, and pressing forward to the mark of the high calling of God in Christ Jesus. (Deliverance → Breakthrough → Renewal.)

We are now moving forward to repentance. We are pursuers of peace and holiness. As Tim Tenney says, we are God chasers. We're not hiding anymore. We believe God will fulfill his promise and finish what he has started in us. "I will put my Spirit in you and you will live" (Ezekiel 37:14)—a life of breakthroughs!

God's relationship with us is a continual thing. You know that, right? Our response shows up when we move as a result of God's call to begin in repentance, the call to believe, the call to build up our faith and become true disciples. God calls us to be in service, to respond to the voice of the Spirit, and to lay down our lives for the needs of others.

Think of God's call as continually twofold. It is a call to be saved people and to be saving people. It is a call to be forgiven and to forgive those who share our same need. Someone said God's call, for all you NASCAR fans, is like riding on a high-banked oval. Our life accelerates and speeds up when we come out of God's call, when we move in response to God's call upon our lives.

We used to have a Hot Wheels ® toy when I grew up called the Super Charger. It was a battery-operated machine with turnstiles that spun on both sides of the track. The turnstiles whirled around propelling the car that passed through down the track. We prayed it wouldn't throw the car off the first curve it went around. The cars would coast around the track and come back through, and zoom! The car shot out and sped around the track again. The car had to stay on the track for the Super Charger to work. It is the same way with God. As we move forward, catapulted towards repentance or service we have to stay on track to be any good.

Now, we have gained access to the power to do a whole lot of good. Our minds are renewed in step with God's mercies. We follow the pathway of grace. This path begins in God's deliverance and our repentance. Then we are moved toward breakthroughs: "aha" moments, where we see "Wow, that is how I move forward with God." And then we are again renewed by God.

More and more, our way becomes clarified and energized by God's call upon our lives. We're pressing on to live as we are loved, to know we are known.

God has come into our lives. God has touched us and said, "You're it!" Now, we are forever in pursuit of God. Paul comes to Miletus having called for the elders of the Ephesus church to meet him there (Acts 20:17–35). With deep love and concern, Paul maps out the course of action he had taken with them. Now we will see how what he shared with them is also meant for our good.

Pay attention to where you are. Walk the path as you follow each map. Begin in repentance. Believe your way from where you are to where you were meant to be. Build up your faith and develop the skills each map shares. Be blessed. You are being made into a greater blessing for others. Bring life. Use what you know and learn. Breakthrough!

Let's map out the course our lives of breakthrough will take. The Apostle Paul will be God's cartographer, God's map maker. I will transcribe the details. The distance or scale each map covers is our lifetime. Our true north is Jesus. We begin with Jesus. We move with Jesus. Our final destination is matching our every step with his.

The pathway of grace will be our template. We will use it to draw four maps. Read through all four, and then decide which one was made for you. (See Appendix E for a fuller, more detailed description for each map.) The four maps correspond to the four ways we can be rooted in sin. As I told you in the introduction of this book, we have all sinned. We have all been rooted in expressing our life that has its point of origin in sin. For some of us, that expression shows up in the way we feel rejected or in the things we reject. We betray God's expectations for us or our own expectations and fall short (Map 1).

Others of us aggressively or passively express themselves by doing what they like to do. We are biased. We have a way we prefer. It is our way. Our weaknesses reveal themselves through an over reliance on our "strengths." We over rely on our way. To speak of ourselves as right-handed or left-handed is not to say I have inferior muscles on one side of my body, so I rely on this side. It just means I'm used to using one side more than the other. We respond to different situations, and we come into conflict because we insist on our "dominant" way of doing things. We come into conflict because we won't adapt our way to allow another way to be used. We always insist on our own way (Map 2).

Others of us feel entitled to have grace come our way. We would be just as happy to get an excuse for our sin as forgiveness. It's not our fault anyway. If things were fair, things would be equal, and we would be fine (Map 3).

Others of us are doing the best we can. If there was a better way, we would have tried it. Things don't work for us like they do for other people. We're not defensive by nature. We're defensive by necessity. You would know that if you had been through what we have (Map 4).

Paul's final message to the elders of the church in Ephesus (Acts 20:17–35) outlines the course of action he took with them and provides the demonstration, the map, for their response to God's grace. Paul begins each map with a declaration of how he represented God when he was among the church in Ephesus.

From Miletus, Paul sent to Ephesus for the elders of the church. When they arrived, he said to them: "You know how I lived the whole time I was with you, from the first day I came into the province of Asia. I served the Lord with great humility and with tears, although I was severely tested by the plots of the Jews. You know that I have not hesitated to preach anything that would be helpful to you but have taught you publicly and from house to house. I have declared to both Jews and Greeks that they must turn to God in repentance and have faith in our Lord Jesus. And now, compelled by the Spirit, I am going to Jerusalem, not knowing what will happen to me there. I only know that in every city the Holy Spirit warns me that prison and hardships are facing me. However, I consider my life worth nothing to me, if only I may finish the race and complete the task the Lord Jesus has given me—the task of testifying to the gospel of God's grace. Now I know that none of you among whom I have gone about preaching the kingdom will ever see me again. Therefore, I declare to you today that I am innocent of the blood of all men. For I have not hesitated to proclaim to you the whole will of God. Keep watch over yourselves and all the flock of which the Holy Spirit has made you overseers. Be shepherds of the church of God, which he bought with his own blood. I know that after I leave, savage wolves will come in among you and will not spare the flock. Even from your own number men will arise and distort the truth in order to draw away disciples after them. So be on your guard! Remember that for three years I never stopped warning each of you night and day with tears. Now I commit you to God and to the word of his grace, which can build you up and give you an inheritance among all those who are sanctified. I have not coveted anyone's silver or gold or clothing. You yourselves know that these hands of mine supplied my own needs and the needs of my companions. In everything I did, I showed you that by this kind of hard work we must help the weak, remembering the words the Lord Jesus himself said: 'It is more blessed to give than to receive.'"

For those following Map 1, Paul reminds us God's faithfulness includes God's faith in us. God is becoming our servant believing in us and loving us into a place of mastery. Paul's service to the church at Ephesus represented this disposition of God that says, "I am here for you. I will not leave you or forsake you. I will be your confidence. I will be your driving force, your mainstay, your friend."

Those following Map 2 will begin where Map 1 ends. As you read these verses of scripture in Acts 20, you will notice these maps convey the attitudes, the skills, and the knowledge under which we need to live for a life of breakthrough.

Paul reminds those following Map 2 that God's way is always more enjoyable and enduring than our own. Because God wants us to succeed in receiving and sharing the fullness of grace, God will persist in attesting to the overabundance of the way he is for us through his Son Jesus Christ.

When we try to outthink God, God will remind us he can do abundantly above what we can ask or think. Followers of Map 3 realize when we put our trust in God, we not only receive the testimony that reveals the superiority of God's way to ours, God asks us to concur to that way through our own testimony.

We also can get rooted in blaming others or in the way we are unable or unwilling to forgive. We turn ourselves into victims. We don't take responsibility for what is going on in our lives. Our path toward freedom from blame will be revealed in Map 3.

The final way of expressing sin shows itself in bitterness. We know the world is against us, and there's not a lot we can do about it. We will have to keep on being ourselves. Unfortunately, being ourselves right now means being defined more by our hurts than our hopes, more by our wounds than by God's way of forgiveness and healing.

But, we do not despair. Why? God will be a true father to us. God will insist that we revel in the rewards of grace. In order to do that, we will have to respond in responsibility to the grace we have already been given.

Those following Map 4, God wants to make your life new altogether. God comes to us and tells us he knows our heart. God will not sit idly by and let grace come to nothing in us. God will be our teacher, our nanny, our physical therapist. God will bring us along beside himself and stretch us and train us back to a place of wholeness.

Our conversion, not our comfort, will be God's priority. God will draw close to us, unsettling perhaps in his closeness. God will say, "No matter what, I want you to choose to cling to me so that when all is said and done your movements can match up to mine."

Follow the direction of the maps and you will find yourself transformed more and more into the glorious likeness of Jesus.

Map 1 (Acts 20:17–21)

1. We begin in humility that reins us in under God's control. We are who we are by the grace of God. Our choices and failures to choose are not what define us. What God says about us is what we accept, in humility, as true.

2. We believe everything about us and our circumstances can change. Our tears magnify God's work in our lives and show our appreciation of the fact that God has the last word on us.

3. We build up our faith by enduring the tests we face. Usually this will involve admitting our mistakes quickly, allowing others to help us, forsaking our procrastination, and humbling ourselves on a regular basis.

4. We bless others by making good decisions, setting aside our hesitancy and our fears.

5. We bring life by being the same humble follower of Jesus whether in public or private.

6. We breakthrough when our life is an open display of repentance and faith.

Map 2 (Acts 20:21–24)

1. We begin with reliance upon God and his Word that trumps our doubts and rationalizations.

2. We believe Jesus is Lord over our heart, soul, mind, and

strength. We know obedience is more important than our convenience or our experience.

3. We build up our strength by being compelled by the Holy Spirit. Being intelligent and pragmatic is good. Being intelligent, pragmatic, and full of faith is far better and can accomplish far more.

4. We bless others by offering our faith and expertise in a spirit of cooperation and charity. We are learning how to move forward even when we don't control all the variables.

5. We bring life when we serve others with joy and demonstrate the character of Jesus in every task we complete. We bring life when we see serving with others as a vocation.

5. We breakthrough when our life is a testimony to God's grace more than a recognition of our skill and vision.

Map 3 (Acts 20:25–32)

1. We begin in repentance by responding to situations in innocence. We do not assign blame or guilt to others. We forgive and accept full responsibility for our lives.

2. We believe in being forthright. We believe Jesus alone is always reliable. We can admit our shortcomings and accept others in theirs.

3. We build up our faith by holding a positive but realistic outlook for ourselves. We know that God is always working things together for our good and that the last word is his. We will not be drained or weakened by criticism or criticizing.

4. We bless others by nourishing, encouraging, and educating others into their best. We bless as directly as possible, so we lead by example.

5. We bring life by humbly reminding others how the truth can be distorted. We warn of the dangers that come from putting too much trust in people rather than God, in man-made systems rather than Jesus our Savior.

6. We breakthrough when we commend others not to see things our way but to see and follow the Word of God's grace for their lives.

Map 4 (Acts 20:32–35)

1. We begin in repentance by resigning ourselves to the Word of God's grace. Our pain, resentment, justifications, and explanations are all relinquished to God's redemptive power.

2. We believe and are determined to reveal God's grace is sufficient for our weakness. We believe we can find restoration and healing and that it is God's holy will to give it to us.

3. We build up our faith by investing our time and energy in what will meet our needs and the needs of others.

4. We bless others by working hard. We are called to be a blessing. We do not lay guilt trips on others or call attention to our own needs.

5. We bring life by giving as God in Christ has generously given grace to us.

6. We breakthrough when others remember the words and works of Jesus, when they hear or see ours.

Are you following your map? (See Appendix F for a fuller, more detailed description of the maps.)

A GIFT FOR YOUR JOURNEY

God has always meant for you to live up to the speed of his grace. "And I heard a loud voice from the throne saying, 'Now the dwelling of God is with men, and he will live with them. They will be his people and God himself will be with them and be their God'" (Revelation 21:3). Over and over again, the scripture says we shall be like him. Jesus confessed we would do greater works than he did because the Holy Spirit would live and move through us. All of this is God's gift and promise.

Jesus said, "I will be with you always" (Matthew 28:20). Our life of breakthrough is simply the revelation of that truth. To move at the speed of grace is to follow Jesus—not from a distance, not inconsistently, but in communion of heart and soul.

How do we achieve that consistency? The number one thing we can do is practice following Jesus. Follow with others who share a like, precious faith. Use this book in a Bible study or small group. Pray. Read the scriptures until they revolutionize the way you see the world. Serve the needs of others. Exert your energy and influence into things that bring you and others fullness of life. I think I've found around forty-five places in scripture and life where the pathway of grace is written or fleshed out. I'm hoping you'll find some examples I haven't found yet.

The number one thing you will need to practice following Jesus is the presence and power of the Holy Spirit. Get thirsty for the Holy Spirit. Then, ask Jesus to fill you and refill you. Be specific and ask Jesus for the gift that draws you into constant alignment with God. Ask and you will receive. Ask for the gift of grace that the Apostle Paul calls godly sorrow. I call it God-grief.

God-grief enables our spirits to be linked with God's Spirit. Our conscience is its shadow and is substantiated by this gift. When we experience God-grief, we feel and see things as God does. We are God-empathizers. We appreciate the work of God and focus on it so that it becomes our work. We agree with Jesus: "My food is to do the will of him who sent me and to finish his work" (John 4:34).

It is God-grief because it works us down to repentance. It brings us to acknowledge our sin and align ourselves with Jesus, leading to salvation. The counterfeit, worldly sorrow or cosmic-grief works us down to regret. We regret being a sinner, and we align ourselves with others, leading us to contradictions. We demand change while insisting on acceptance. No wonder the more things change the more things stay the same.

God-grief moves us to acknowledge the distinctions between our way and God's and to move us as quickly as possible to reconcile the two. Cosmic-grief moves us to blur or deny the distinctions, moving us as quickly as possible to justify ourselves in whatever position we occupy.

God-grief inspired the title of this book: *Moving at the Speed of Grace*. God-grief produces something in us. It works a change in us recognizable in repentance.

What does God-grief produce? It produces speed. It produces speed to walk the pathway of grace. Allow it to work in your mind. What will it produce? The Apostle Paul spells it out in 2 Corinthians 7:10–11. It provides speed to:

1. Begin in repentance and align ourselves with God, to give an account and apology to God of our actions. It accelerates us into repentance.

2. Believe and resonate with God's will. We suffer grief in any distance between our will and God's, accelerating us into believing in faith for all God wants for us.

3. Build up our faith conforming us to God's best while cautioning us against the world's worst. God-grief sets the alarms off in our spirit, soul, and body causing us to live in the fear of the Lord. It accelerates us into building up our faith.

4. Bless others, to desire and obsess over God's best for ourselves and others. God-grief gives us focus to dote upon solutions to problems that will bless others.

5. Bring life. We can affect change that benefits others as well as ourselves. God-grief sustains our zeal, causing grace to boil over from us bringing life to others.

6. Breakthrough and finish what we start. God-grief works to vindicate the enduring mercy and justice of God.

Ask God for this gift. Ask Jesus to let you see things as he sees them. Ask Jesus to let you feel things as he feels them. Ask Jesus to move you as he moves. Ask and receive the gift that reconciles your way to God's. Receive the gift of God-grief.

I've known I needed this gift for a long time. Watching a loved one act and speak inappropriately as he got older moved me to pray this prayer. "Lord, work your Spirit into me, so when I am not myself, I look more like you than me." You see, whenever my loved one used angry or vulgar speech, the caregiver would forgive and excuse the behavior saying, "He's not himself." I had my suspicions, so I more resolutely prayed my prayer.

I want to be like Jesus who was always himself "the same yesterday, today, and forever" (Hebrews 13:8). I want to live a no excuse, no regret kind of life. I receive the gift of God-grief. I allow it to produce speed in my spirit to match the movement of God's Spirit.

I struggled for years with handling administrative tasks in an appropriate way. In seminary, tested for our strengths in ministry, I received a crushing confirmation of my weakness. Out of a possible score of a hundred, I received an eight in the area of administration.

I was in my first church appointment, and the time came for our annual church conference. I was to assemble a multitude of reports for the two churches I served and present them in a cohesive manner in front of my congregations to my supervisor, the district superintendent.

I had one big problem. I didn't know how to ready these forms and make the report. I asked members of my church who were chairpersons of the committees for which the reports were designated, but they were as clueless as I was. They told me, "I just sign the forms. The preacher always fills it out." This preacher didn't know how to fill them out.

I called the district superintendent and told him I wouldn't be ready. He assured me I would be. The night arrived for the meeting, and I proved myself right. What followed was a humiliating evening of being told in front of my parishioners that I would never make a good pastor if this was the best I could do. I was inclined to agree.

For almost twenty years, this season of the year, my favorite time growing up became a time of dread for me. It was the season to be proven inadequate again. That is, until I finally saw the situation as God saw it and God-grief began to produce speed in facing this responsibility head on.

The change took place on my first trip to Brazil. The pathway of grace was coming into focus, and I knew that I was saved by God for a life of breakthroughs, not for a series of break downs. I asked God how I was going to handle this situation, this annual church conference, in a way that showed his grace was greater than my eight.

It was then I sensed God asking me questions.

"Norm, are you a Christian?"

"Yes, Lord, you know I am a Christian."

"Norm, have you put your trust in my Son, Jesus?"

"Yes, you know that I trust you, Lord."

"Now, Norm, do you believe when you put your trust in me that I poured out my Holy Spirit into you?"

"Yes, Lord, I believe you did."

"Well, Norm, don't you think my Holy Spirit is a pretty good administrator?"

"Yes, Lord, you can manage the whole universe. You uphold everything with the word of your power."

"Good, let me uphold you. Let my Holy Spirit work through you, and as an added bonus, people will start giving you credit for being a good administrator."

This is something of the dialogue God and I had that day. All I truly remember was the deep sense of peace that came over me. The gut-wrenching turmoil of the past was replaced with a deep, abiding confidence that I could handle things differently now. I knew I was adequate to the task. I was up to speed and moving at the speed of grace.

How? I humbled myself and acknowledged my sin of rejecting and betraying what God said about me. I began to appreciate with tears how I could trust God for everything inwardly and outwardly I needed for the church conference. The indwelling Holy Spirit gave me the administrative strength to face and overcome the test the conference had always been for me. I made the decision: I'm doing what needs to be done on time and without anxiety. I knew this job could be accomplished like all other jobs. I had God's smile.

I know there are challenges ahead, but I know God and I are up for it. I know the same is true of you. I know "as you learn more and more how God works, you will learn how to do your work" (Colossians 1:10, *The Message*), the work of moving at the speed of grace!

SMALL GROUP DISCUSSION QUESTIONS

1. What breakthroughs have you had in your life?

2. Which one of the four maps do you need to have a breakthrough? Map 1–I am not worthy to be God's servant; Map 2–My way is the best way and only way; Map 3–It is not my fault because life is not fair; or Map 4–I am doing the very best I can at this time.

3. Now look at the steps for your map. Discuss with your

group how to walk through these steps. Imagine what it would be like to walk these steps and have a breakthrough in your walk with God.

4. Where do you feel that God is asking you to grow at this time? How will you do that? What is your first step to take? Share this with your group.

Our First Parents and the Pathway of Sin

As we begin this journey together, I will focus on the pathway of God's grace. I will expect the Holy Spirit to turn you onto that path. I will expect the Holy Spirit to mark your exit from the pathway of sin. For now let's review our first parents' story. The way sin worked in them is still the way sin works in us. The good news that you will see over and over again in this book is that God has provided us a way out of sin, a pathway of grace.

Put yourself in Adam and Eve's shoes for a minute. Go back and read Genesis, chapters 3–4. Sin begins in betrayal. Sin is a breach in trust. That locks us into a self-serving bias. Proverbs 3:5–7 offers us a clear path for reconciling ourselves to God and the pathway of grace. "Trust in the Lord with all your heart; lean not unto your own understanding. In all your ways acknowledge him and he will direct your paths. Be not wise in your own eyes. Fear the Lord and depart from evil."

Repair the breach. Acknowledge the betrayal by hightailing it to God. Don't lean to your own understanding. Don't substantiate the temptation. "The woman saw that the fruit of the tree was good for food and pleasing to the eye, and also desirable for gaining wisdom" (Genesis 3:6). Of course, this was true. The tree was good because God is good. That doesn't make it your tree. I have peach trees and apple trees in my orchard at home. The fruit is good and tastes great. I live an hour away. Do I want everyone who admires the fruitfulness of my trees to have some? No, I'd prefer to eat it myself or, at the very least, be asked for permission.

Adam and Eve did none of this. They could have exerted a little faith in God during this temptation. "Serpent, what you say sounds pretty good. We'll check it with God when we walk with him this evening. Come back tomorrow, or better yet, hang around until God gets here. We'll give you a tour of the rest of the garden while we wait."

Even after the sin occurred, Adam and Eve could have moved in grace to begin in repentance with God. Instead, they hid themselves. Proverbs 3 commands us to acknowledge God in all our ways. When confronted with his trespass, Adam couldn't acknowledge responsibility for it. Instead, he moved from bias to blame and said, "The woman you put here with me—she gave me some fruit from the tree, and I ate it."

Blame won't hold up. If you have eyes to see, you could move to begin with God again in repentance. Adam could have leaned on God instead of Eve, but Adam did not move quickly or hightail it to begin again with God. Adam moved quickly and immediately to blame.

Go a little further into the scripture. The next stage of sin unfolds. The curse has come. Cain and Abel bring a sacrifice to God. Cain's sacrifice is of his own making. He knows how to make it better—acceptable to God. Cain chooses being bitter over being better. God warns Cain, "Why are you angry? Why is your face downcast? If you do what is right, will you not be accepted? But, if you do not do what is right, sin is crouching at your door; it desires to master you, but you must master it" (Genesis 4:6–7).

Proverbs 3 promises God will warn us. God will give us a path of mastery in grace—a path of breakthrough. "God will direct our paths."

Sin desires mastery over you. Bitterness will beget bloodshed in us as it did in Cain. That's why Proverbs 3 calls us out of this cycle of violence when it says, "Be not wise in your own eyes. Fear the Lord and depart from evil." It's not all about you or me. The world doesn't revolve around us. When it does, someone goes down. Bloodshed moves us to a breaking point of judgment.

What has happened to all of us? We have sinned and sin has brought death to our lives. Now, we didn't stop breathing when we first sinned. No, we died to who we were created to be—living, breathing signs of grace. We died to living a spirit filled life. We got rooted in expressing our lives with its point of origin in sin. It's now time to get things turned around. It's time to focus on God's point of origin for us: Jesus.

Outlines of the Paths

THE PATH OF SIN

1. Betrayal
2. Bias
3. Blame
4. Bitterness
5. Bloodshed
6. Breaking point/ Break down

THE PATHWAY OF GRACE

1. Begin in repentance
2. Believe
3. Build up your faith
4. Bless
5. Bring Life
6. Breakthrough

THE SHAPE OF SIN

1. Betrayal
2. Bias
3. Blame
4. Bitterness
5. Bloodshed
6. Breaking point/ Break down

THE SOLUTION OF GRACE (PROVERBS 3)

1. Hightail it to the Lord
2. Lean not unto your own understanding
3. In all your ways, acknowledge God
4. He will direct your paths
5. Be not wise in your own eyes
6. Fear the Lord and depart from evil

The Three Temptations

We are going to walk the pathway of grace together. Let me warn you. I have discovered in the writing of this book three great temptations we all face.

1. The first temptation is to maintain the status quo. From the very beginning of creation, from the instant sin entered into the world, we have tried to hide from God, to maintain the distance that sin created. The God who loves us cannot allow that distance to become the status quo. This is the reason Adam and Eve were banished from the garden. If they had eaten from the tree of life, they would have perpetuated their status as sinners. God's work for us and in us always allows for a redo.

    Newton's first law of motion states objects at rest remain at rest and objects in motion remain in motion unless acted upon by an outside force. The first temptation is to let the law instead of grace say who we are. Objects, human beings, all tend to stay how we are unless, as Newton puts it, we are acted upon by an outside force. Put nicely, we are tempted to live and let live. Said not so nicely, we don't want anybody messing with us. We assert the status quo should be good enough. We are resistant to change. The idea of an object resisting change in its motion is called *inertia*. All objects have inertia. The larger the mass of an object, the more inertia it has. Sometimes the greater mess of an object the more inertia it has.

I warn you of this temptation because it's real. The temptation to stay as we are keeps us from backing up or beginning in repentance with God. We justify ourselves and continue to miss the turn that would take us home. Jesus comes to us and we insist he leave us alone.

2. The second temptation I have discovered is jumping track. We say we want to do what's good, but we never lay the axe to the root of our sin. This is why repentance is so important. This is why you can't begin any other way. You cannot jump from walking the path of sin, jumping over to doing what you want to do on the pathway of grace. God requires us to walk humbly with him not teleport into the situations and places we want to visit.

Jumping track, refusing to begin in repentance, will make you a contradiction. How? You can only produce results out of what you are rooted. Jesus said, "Either make the tree good, and its fruit good; or else make the tree corrupt, and its fruit corrupt: for the tree is known by its fruit" (Matthew 12:33).

A person with a root of bitterness once asked, "How come when I say something, no one wants to do it, but if so and so says the same thing, everybody thinks it's a great idea?" I wanted to tell her it's not the idea that's the problem. What we are rooted to has to change if we want our results to change. That change occurs only as we move back to begin in repentance.

Jumping track causes our blessings to be received as curses, our building up or encouragement of another to feel like we're tearing others down, and stating what we believe sounds like we are asserting our superiority.

Jumping track will tempt us to affirm we can live a good life apart from God. Those who jump track will say the best we can do is the best we can do. They never allow themselves to experience a dynamic relationship with God. They will judge people holier-than-thou who testify that an intimate, interactive relationship with God is possible.

Have you ever had a conversation with someone and not understood what they were talking about? They jumped into the conversation at the halfway point of their thoughts instead of the beginning. The great point they wanted to convey sailed over your head. The story they wanted to tell had no foundation to warrant your interest. This is what a life looks like when it jumps track.

Be aware of this temptation. I mentioned it near the end of chapter two.

3. The third temptation, I have observed, draws us to skip or shortcut any part of the path God follows. This is similar to jumping track. Jumping track is primarily skipping repentance and saying if we believe or generally do the right things, we can be right with God. This third temptation is choosing to skip over another stage along the pathway of grace.

This may describe the person who calls on God and goes to church, studies the Bible, prays, etc. but never trusts their lives to the reality of God. This may describe the person who makes a commitment of faith but never or rarely builds up that faith. They just want to be helpful. This may describe the person who likes to be helpful but jumps from one project to the next never getting close to anyone, never investing themselves in or with others. This may describe the person who is faithful but always sells themselves short.

I trust you will become more aware of where you are as we proceed. I explained in chapter ten how this third temptation once trapped and disabled me. The good news is our Deliverer is near. Our Savior is ready to demonstrate how to move at the speed of grace. Are you ready? Get set. Follow Jesus!

Reading for Revolution

There is a practice of reading the scripture I want you to try. Designate a portion of scripture you have time to read each day. I recommend the book of First John. There are certainly other places that could come later: Matthew 5–7, Philippians, Colossians, or a section of scripture you've always found difficult to understand or fit together with other scripture.

You begin reading for revolution by reading your assigned passage every day for thirty days. There may be days when this is difficult. It may seem needlessly repetitious, but persevere. Your spirit will be given the opportunity to make a deep connection to the Holy Spirit. Your spirit will be encouraged. "Finally, he's giving me some regular attention."

This is the first cycle. You have made a good start. Your spirit will be revived.

Begin another thirty-day cycle. Stay focused on the same passage of scripture. Ask God to reveal his way to you. Do not get bored. Your mind will question your activity. "Why are you still reading the same old thing? I know this already."

Keep on reading. It's the only way to prove to your mind that

God has more to reveal. Stay intentional. You are working toward a fundamental transformation of how you think and feel. Your soul is being reshaped by the Scriptures. Concentrating on First John as our first passage of focus realizes the promise of Hebrews 9:14: the blood of Christ will cleanse our conscience from acts that lead to death.

These second thirty days complete the second cycle. Your spirit is well fed. Your soul is strengthened in alignment with the Word, but there is another move towards maturity that you must make.

Read the passage for thirty more days. Why? You are being sanctified spirit, soul, and body. Hebrews 5:13–14 says, "For everyone who partakes only of milk is unskilled in the word of righteousness, for he is still a baby. But solid food is for the mature, which by constant use have their senses exercised to discern both good and evil."

These final thirty days is when the revolution occurs. You will not have to think things through to know whether something is good or evil. You won't have to wait for your spirit to be grieved or encouraged. Your body will react subconsciously as it would if your hand was approaching a hot stove or a dangerous object.

I can testify. I was almost finished reading my final thirty days of First John. I was passing through the living room, and the television was on. Something was said, and before I mentally had time to register that the words from the television didn't agree with the word of First John, my body had recoiled away from it.

This is the goal of Reading for Revolution: that we will move with the good and away from the evil without having to think about it first. It is fine if we have to explain our reasons later, but we want to explain from a position of having done the right thing than having to apologize or extricate ourselves from doing wrong. We don't want to be jerked back and forth between grace and sin. We want to be constantly moving at the speed of grace!

Directions for a Life of Breakthrough

Paul walks through the way he had been with the church at Ephesus. As he reiterates his actions, Paul lays out God's directions for them. Paul details the attitudes, skills, and knowledge needed by each person to live a life of breakthrough. The attitudes describe the particular way we may need to repent and believe. The skills we will develop characterize the method for building up our faith and blessing others that we will follow. The knowledge under which we move forward encompasses the way God calls us to bring life and breakthrough for ourselves and for others. Travel well.

MAP 1

God has a vision for us, and he lays it out here (Acts 20:18–21) to follow:

> When they arrived, he said to them: "You know how I lived the whole time I was with you, from the first day I came into the province of Asia. I served the Lord with great humility and with

tears, although I was severely tested by the plots of the Jews. You know that I have not hesitated to preach anything that would be helpful to you but have taught you publicly and from house to house. I have declared to both Jews and Greeks that they must turn to God in repentance and have faith in our Lord Jesus Christ.

Our service for the Lord ascends from our attitude. Our attitude is one of humility. We are reined in under the guiding hand of God. Our humility arises out of God's predisposition in Jesus Christ to give us all that we need. Paul shares with these same elders in the book of Ephesians, "God will equip us with every spiritual blessing in Christ" (Ephesians 1:3).

This means every way in which we need to be blessed or be a blessing is covered by God's kingdom authority and power. God is on our side. There is no opinion, lie, circumstance, or weapon formed against us that can prosper. There is nothing that can overcome the claim God makes upon our humble heart.

God has chosen us in Christ, even before the creation of the world, to be holy and blameless in his sight. God loves us. God has predestined us to be adopted as his sons through Jesus Christ with all the rights and privileges that go with it.

That is good news. It is no wonder our attitude is one of humility. We are filled with gratitude and fervor for what God has chosen to do for us. God says this is one of my requirements—walk humbly with me.

This attitude of humility flows into the second attitude of appreciation that allows tears to be brought forth out of our life. Tears don't come because we are wimps. We stand amazed and in awe of God's goodness. Some of us feel this way every Sunday night if we watch *Extreme Makeover: Home Edition.* They are building a house, and we sit on the sofa saying, "Don't move the bus, I'll just cry that much more."

Think about the movie *It's a Wonderful Life.* I don't have to watch the whole movie. I'll admit it. I cry. The reason the tears come is I am ready, even if the movie is just starting, for the outpouring of love that's given to George and Mary Bailey at the end of the movie. I'm ready for George's brother, their friends, and neighbors to toast the life they share together in Bedford Falls.

Have you seen the movie? Watch it. I'm ready for the sheriff to tear up the arrest warrant and join in singing the Christmas hymns. I'm ready for the bank examiner to join in, too. I'm ready for the bell to ring and know the angel Clarence got his wings.

Tears are a way of praising God for the glory and freedom of his grace. Our attitude reveals we know what the end will be. We know God is going to work it out. We want the end to come.

We are like a groom that sees his bride for the first time. Our tears are a reflection of her beauty. Our tears spill out in amazement. How did we ever get so blessed to marry her? Of course, we want her to come on down the aisle and stand beside us.

A guy really would cry if his bride showed up at the back door of the church, and the preacher leaned over to him and whispered to him, "This is as close as you will ever get." God forbid. The guy really would cry.

We cry because we know she's coming down the aisle. In just a minute we will join hands. We will declare our intentions. We are going to share our vows and make the pledge of our union known to everybody. We'll even paint it on our car, "Just Married!"

Now, we uphold these attitudes of humility and appreciation. Our tears express how good God is and the end of all things is going to be good as well. We trust God. Maybe, this coming year on our anniversary we will paint "Still Married" on our car.

We are unashamed. Our attitude is the same as the groom's. We are married to God. Tears become the defining witness to the necessity of each person coming to that place where they pledge their faith to God. As the bride and groom join hands together, our lives are joined to God's through Jesus Christ.

These tears well up from within as an expression of God's pleasure and will. It's our way of saying, "God so loved the world that he gave his only begotten son that whosoever believes in him will not perish but have everlasting life" (John 3:16).

One of my favorite preachers when I was growing was known for his tears. Omar Burnett was known as a weeping preacher. He wept because he was convinced God loved everybody to whom he was preaching. I can remember him walking the aisles of the church, looking upon a particular person, and pleading with them with many tears to be reconciled to God.

This attitude doesn't mean we go around crying all the time. It just means our compassion and concern is allowed to rise to the surface. We are unashamed of who we married. We are unashamed of Christ. We are living fully in the present. We have no regrets. Our tears have accessed a vision of God's future.

Our attitude of appreciation allows a holy boldness to emerge, a boldness manifest through our tears. These attitudes of humility and appreciation need to be in place to undergird the skills we need to develop.

The first skill is learning how to endure the tests of life. The Bible teaches that in the last days, the love of many will grow cold, and hearts will grow weak and faint. They haven't developed the skill of enduring tests.

I pray you will ask God in every way you need it, to teach you to endure. Is it in how your money is spent? Is it in your appetites? Can you keep your cool? Do you study the Scriptures? Are you a praying person?

We're not asking God to lead us into temptation but to lead us to know how to face temptation resolutely and responsibly. T. Harv Eker, in *Secrets of a Millionaire Mind,* shares how we need to develop as a person from being, let's say, a number four person with number seven kind of problems to a number eight kind of person who, if having number seven kind of problems is just fine. Hey, I'm a number eight. My problems are sitting at number seven. I can handle that. It's below me. It's when our problems grow big enough to overshadow us we forget God overshadows all of our problems.

We develop the skill of handling adversity, the skill of enduring problems. It may mean we fail. But we don't give up. We don't quit. We don't say, "That's just something I can't do." We may say, "It's something I can't do today, but tomorrow I'll try again. I'll know how to handle it differently. I'll hit it at a different angle tomorrow. I'll consider it from a different viewpoint."

It's said that Thomas Edison was once asked while trying to invent a working light bulb, "How do you deal with these thousands and thousands of failures?" Edison is reputed to have said, "I've never had a failure, but I've had thousands and thousands of successes in showing me how not to make a light bulb." So, we develop the skill of enduring tests, even those, as Paul experienced, thrust upon us by our brothers.

The other skill we develop is how to be a person who is—this is hard for those of us who don't come to this naturally—decisive. We develop the skill of making decisions, the skill of going ahead, the skill of finishing something.

I'm so glad there are people in my life who are good at finishing things. They are good at making decisions. I was raised in a family of indecisive people.

"Where do y'all want to go to supper tonight?" "Oh, I don't know. Whatever is fine with me." There is no "Whatever" restaurant in town. Back and forth my family would go. It's a good thing there weren't many options to choose from when we grew up. We would have starved or still be driving around.

God says if you want to live a life of breakthrough and not break down there is something you are going to have to begin to do better. Make decisions. Live with them. If they are wrong, you say, "That was wrong. I should have done that differently. I should have handled that test differently." And you do.

You see, God says there are some things I want you to know. Two things, the Apostle Paul gives here for those who follow Map 1.

We know we need to be the same person in public as in private or in private as we are in public. In God's eyes we should say and do the same kinds of things whether we are not being observed at all or 50,000 people are looking at us.

We are just as willing to say "Jesus is Lord" to a good friend as we are if we are brought before the tribunal to be questioned. Paul says, "You know that I have not hesitated to preach anything that would be helpful to you, but have taught you [I've done the same thing] publicly and from house to house" (Acts 20:20).

The final thing we know and declare is that everybody needs to turn to God in repentance and have faith in our Lord Jesus Christ. That's just the way it is. It is a need everybody has. I have that need. You have that need. Everybody has that need. They must turn to God in repentance and have faith in our Lord Jesus Christ.

I warn you in the fear of the Lord, don't do as some already have—using God's map to scribble out their own, exchanging the universal call to repentance unto salvation for their more enlightened universal call to salvation.

Don't go into what God calls you to do and try to offer your objections ahead of your obedience. You know God. If you have questions, then ask for help to work it out as you follow. Do not start a detour before starting the journey. Our attitude is expressed through humility and appreciative tears. We are learning how to endure the tests of life. We exercise the skill of taking decisive steps for God. We know we need to be the same public or private. We know we need to be that way because whether we are in public or private there will not be a single person in front of us who doesn't need to turn to God in repentance and have faith in Jesus Christ.

MAP 2

Again I remind you, Paul is mapping out the attitudes, skills, and knowledge needed by each person to live a life of breakthrough. The attitudes describe the particular way we need to repent and believe. The skills we develop characterize the method for building up our faith and blessing others. The knowledge under which we move forward encompasses the way God calls us to bring life and breakthrough for ourselves and for others. Keep it mind, and keep your eyes on the road ahead.

> I have declared to both Jews and Greeks that they must turn to God in repentance and have faith in our Lord Jesus Christ. And now, compelled by the Spirit, I am going to Jerusalem, not knowing what will happen to me there. I only know that in every city the Holy Spirit warns me that prison and hardships are facing me. However, I consider my life worth nothing to me, if only I may finish the race and complete the task the Lord Jesus has given me—the task of testifying to the gospel of God's grace.
>
> Acts 20:21–24

An attitude of reliance ushers the follower of Map 2 onto the right path. The wise man of Proverbs says this reliance is in the Lord. "Trust in the Lord with all your heart and lean not unto your own understanding. In all your ways acknowledge him and he shall direct your paths" (Proverbs 3:5–6).

This reliance is built on following the voice of the Holy Spirit. The Spirit's voice is the first voice for which we listen. We become the little child who was given great advice in elementary school: "Go with your first thought."

Now, as an adult, we will have to remind ourselves that we are making decisions based on our reliance in God. Rationalizations, reasoning, predetermined opinions are being consciously muted. This exercise in repentance will be repeated over and over again.

Rely on Jesus. This is your attitude. Rely on wells of living water springing up from within you. Rely on your faith producing joy. Your new motto is: "Weeping may endure for a night but joy cometh in the morning" (Psalm 30:5, KJV). Your attitude of solely relying on your own reason or experience has been exchanged. You are expanding your thinking to now rely upon the faithful providence of God.

All of us have to choose each day which umbrella we will walk under. One umbrella operates under the reign of God's grace. The other umbrella represents sin and the evil that inspires it. Both claim to be a sufficient way of explaining our lives.

Both represent sufficiency. One relies on the fact that Jesus says, "My grace is sufficient for you for my strength is made perfect in your weakness" (2 Corinthians 12:9). The other relies on living with a de facto spiritual uncertainty principle. Jesus alludes to it when he says, "Sufficient unto the day is the evil thereof" (Matthew 6:34, KJV).

One way of relying on God produces intimacy. The other produces a respectful distance that never gets you up to speed with God. Paul demonstrates we can and must put reliance and obedience to Jesus first if we are to live simultaneously as citizens of God's kingdom and citizens of the earth.

To see this choice through, we will add to our reliance on God the attitude of obedience. Paul declares: I am relying on the voice of the Holy Spirit to go to Jerusalem. I am demonstrating my obedience to God in this because I don't know what will happen to me there. The outcome is uncertain in the particulars, but I am sure if I obey more information will be forthcoming.

Sure enough, we can read in Acts 21:8–12 Paul and his traveling companions:

> Reached Caesarea and stayed at the house of Philip the evangelist, one of the Seven. He had four unmarried daughters who prophesied. After we had been there a number of days, a prophet named Agabus came down from Judea. Coming over to us, he took Paul's belt, tied his own hands and feet with it and said, "The Holy Spirit says, 'In this way the Jews of Jerusalem will bind the owner of this belt and will hand him over to the Gentiles.'"

The attitude of obedience has to match the attitude of reliance on God; otherwise, we will always question God instead of following passionately. Without an attitude of obedience, we will pull back when things become difficult or don't make sense. We will be persuaded out of fulfilling God's will.

Paul's friends, on hearing the prophecy, "pleaded with Paul not to go to Jerusalem. Then Paul answered, 'Why are you weeping and breaking my heart? I am ready not only to be bound, but also to die in Jerusalem for the name of the Lord Jesus.' When he would not be dissuaded, we gave up and said, 'The Lord's will be done.' After this, we got ready and went up to Jerusalem" (Acts 21:13–15).

The attitude of reliance must always be yoked to the attitude of obedience. You cannot walk the pathway of grace unless they are joined together. Nowhere is this more graphically illustrated than in 1 Kings 13. Read that chapter and see the life and death reasons why these attitudes are yoked together as you follow Map 2. (If your Bible is not handy, see 1 Kings 13 in Appendix F.)

The attitudes of reliance and obedience enable us to present ourselves to God as a living sacrifice (Romans 12:1–2). They are the prerequisite for the skills we are to develop: learning how to be compelled by the Spirit and how to live with the limitations and restrictions placed on us by others.

The first skill is learning how to be compelled by the Holy Spirit. This is the skill of putting our thoughts and actions into submission to Christ. The key to developing this skill is to remember the overriding goodness of God. Bible study is helpful. Godly counsel and wisdom is even better to remind us. Our own experience of the grace of God is also an encouragement.

You see, when we are compelled by the Spirit, Paul says we will be called into situations and projects where we can't predetermine the outcome. Wisdom beyond ourselves can serve to increase our faith and give us the grace to go ahead rather than pull back and become the master of life evaluation we like to be.

Pride is always shortsighted. Our rebellious hearts must be proven wrong or encouraged that there is a greater vision than our own. Barring that proof, we will only go where we can run the show. My grandfather wrestled with developing this skill. During the Great Depression he had the cash to buy thousands of acres of farmland. He bought a 115-acre farm. His brother bought 110 acres next door. His other brother bought seventy-six acres adjacent to that farm. Did my grandfather not want to have way more than his brothers?

I asked him why he hadn't bought all the parcels and had one big farm. He said he didn't know how he would have worked it all. So, he didn't. He bought 115 acres. Imagine the possibilities. He couldn't. He was a smart man, finished second in his class in college. He was a science and math whiz. But, as far as I know, he never asked anyone familiar with managing a lot of land how he might go about doing it himself. What he didn't know was what he didn't know, so he didn't go there. Off limits were off limits.

He was successful in all that he did. He was a great husband and daddy, a great educator and administrator. He was remembered and honored by all who knew him whether that acquaintance was through his service in the church, or his work in the school or through his years at the Soil Conservation Service.

But, I can imagine how he would have learned to trust God in a greater fashion if this skill had been developed. I can imagine how some of his secret insecurities would have been overcome. I can envision him being the man of peace the same way that his bride of sixty-three years was a woman of peace.

This skill of being compelled by the Spirit is the first step in the two step dance of overcoming our pride and bias. The second step is learning how to live with the limitations and restrictions placed on us by others.

Everyone who follows the compelling lead of God's Spirit will run into opposition. The Apostle Paul is certain of that. "Yes, and all that will live godly in Christ Jesus shall suffer persecution" (2 Timothy 3:12). Why? When you follow God's lead, God makes you a leader. When we follow the pathway of grace and demonstrate the "doctrine, manner of life, purpose, faith, longsuffering, charity, and patience" of God, we will begin to have followers (2 Timothy 3:10, KJV).

Some of those followers will be for us. Some will be against us. We who follow Map 2 will develop the skill of being obedient to God while working with both groups. Paul says in Acts 20:24 that he does not sit down and plan what he is going to do with each group. Paul says he puts no thought into that at all. His focus, the skill he is asking us to develop, is to have clarity in hearing and responding to the Holy Spirit.

Paul says I know this will not make me the favorite guest at the party. Some will not want me to speak lest I speak in the power of the Holy Spirit to their situation. The Rev. Daniel Soares Bonfim was known for having this problem. Rev. Bonfim was a mighty man of God who built and pastored a church of 25,000 in Rio de Janeiro, Brazil.

Compelled by the Spirit, Pastor Bonfim would be given revelation into the hearts of those in his congregation. For those who wished for their sins to be uncovered and forgiven, this revelation was proof that God loved them and cared for them. For those who did not want their sins exposed, this revelation was an invasion of privacy and brought public shame and reproach. Eventually, those who were jealous or angry with Pastor Bonfim's ministry drove him out of the church and had him expelled from the Methodist Conference. Years passed before he was restored and received back.

Most people think you have to plan your words to suit your audience. We dare not offend. Some might think it's absolutely appropriate to turn someone around when they are driving the wrong way on a one-way street. You will honk your horn. You will flash your lights. You may even try to swerve over to awaken them to the fact they are going the wrong way and they might be hurt or hurt someone. When they stop, you find out they were lost and didn't know where they were going. You are so relieved you stopped them and turned them around before they went any further.

Get that same driver out of his car and find out his soul is lost. Most people I know will not find it equally as appropriate to turn them around before they go any further. Most in our day would rather avoid disagreements altogether. Those driving in the right direction should move and give plenty of room to the person going the wrong way. Imagine the thoughts of the person going the wrong way. *Why is everyone so rude? Why is everyone flashing their lights up in my face? Why are they trying to make me wreck?*

Sadly today, the more pleasantly you can say something the more persuasive you become. Pray a pleasant person who is lost never takes the lead. Paul will warn the elders of the church at Ephesus about the deceit that can disguise itself with concern, but for now he knows what he is called to do.

Those who follow Map 2 must know this, as well. We are not people pleasers. We are God pleasers. We have one thing to guarantee: that we finish our course with joy and complete the ministry to which the Lord Jesus has called us.

What is our ministry? We are willing and obedient partners in God working everything together for our good. We know that if we pursue any goal, speak to any concern, we must testify to the gospel of God's grace. Billy Graham was once asked, "Mr Graham, given entrée into the company of so many presidents over the years, why haven't you championed different causes for the good of the country?" The Reverend Graham replied that he hadn't promoted different policies or programs because he had tried to keep himself focused on one cause through the years—the cause of Christ.

If you are following Map 2 you know and remind yourself you have but one cause. You have but one thing to which you bear witness. You testify to the gospel of God's grace.

Jesus condensed these directions down for Peter in John 21:15–22. The attitudes of reliance and obedience are wrapped up in the question, "Simon, son of John, do you love me?" For those following blueprint 2 this is how you judge your attitude. Do you love Jesus? Are you willing to give him the benefit of your doubts and rationalizations? The skills of being compelled by the Holy Spirit and learning to live with the limitations placed on you by others is overcome through feeding Jesus' sheep and tending his lambs. This will bring Simon Peter to a place, Jesus says, where others will dress him and take him where he doesn't want to go, but he will be ready. Jesus says to Peter, "It doesn't matter what others may do or not do. It doesn't matter what God does or doesn't do in others. You have one task. Follow me!"

MAP 3

It doesn't bother me to say it again. We are following the pathway of grace when we follow each map. The attitudes describe the particular way we need to repent and believe. The skills we develop characterize the means by which we build up our faith and bless others. The knowledge under which we move forward encompasses the way God calls us to bring life and live a life of breakthrough. Maps 1 and 2 have shown us how to get along with God. Let's yield the right of way, and let Map 3 begin to show us how to get along with others.

> Now I know that none of you among whom I have gone about preaching the kingdom will ever see me again. Therefore, I declare to you today that I am innocent of the blood of all men. For I have not hesitated to proclaim to you the whole will of God. Keep watch over yourselves and all the flock of which the Holy Spirit has made you overseers. Be shepherds of the church of God, which he bought with his own blood. I know that after I leave, savage wolves will come in among you and will not spare the flock. Even from your own number men will arise and distort the truth in order to draw away disciples after them. So be on your guard! Remember that for three years I never stopped warning each of you night and day with tears. Now I commit you to God and to the word of his grace, which can build you up and give you an inheritance among all those who are sanctified.
>
> Acts 20:25–32

The first attitude of someone following Map 3 is innocence. We don't blame anyone for our situation. We are not looking for excuses. We are responsible for our own lives. We are alert to God, and we alert others when their actions and assumptions lead them astray. Paul said, "I have not hesitated to proclaim to you the whole will of God" (Acts 20:27).

The second attitude is openness. You want the bad with the

good. You want your bias to be revealed. When you go to a restaurant, are you open to everything on the menu? I'm not. I usually pick the restaurant for the item I wish to eat. If I go to eat at a church member's house, I'm praying they prepare their food the way Karen does.

Dr. John Savage often said, "Healthy people always have options. Unhealthy people don't." Unhealthy people naturally limit themselves by their own bias. They can be like the woman I knew whose dislike for doctors kept her at home even though she knew something was terribly wrong with her body. By the time she went, the diagnosis came too late for a cure.

Perhaps you are as pitiful as I've been when going to meet the family of a friend in college. I shunned their supper and said out loud "I don't eat bought ham. I only eat what's been cured in our smokehouse." Without an attitude of openness, you make yourself a small person and move towards the no-option lifestyle of those rooted in bitterness.

Openness allows you to take others seriously while not taking yourself too seriously. Openness means you can stand to have your views tested. It doesn't mean any way is fine, choose your own route. Amazingly, that family and their daughter whom I had disrespected remained my friends and years later my friend's mother rejoiced over me when I ate something green. Also, openness implies I am ready to love you. You are ready to love me until we can find together, as the Apostle Paul put it, the more excellent way.

Without an attitude of openness, you will never adequately develop the skill of keeping watch over yourself and *all* the flock of which the Holy Spirit has made you overseer. Without openness, all will have to see things as you do, or they will become disregarded and ultimately discarded. And, you can't oversee what you've chosen to overlook.

Yes, claim responsible innocence. Do not hesitate to be shaped by the whole truth so help you God. You've got skills to develop.

The Apostle Paul speaks of the first in terms of taking heed to yourself. You have to develop the skill of being objective with yourself. Can you imagine your life as a movie you watch rather than a play you are in? Do you merely react to the words of others or the trials of the day like a puppet on a string? Can you see yourself as a distinct individual?

Do yourself and me a favor. Read Mark 7. Then ask yourself, "Does everything defile me? Do I let what occurs outside of me get inside of me?" How many have heard the term "getting under my skin"? Jesus said nothing can do that unless we let it. An oft-used phrase we heard in our house was, "You're about to pluck my last nerve." Well, nerves are under the skin.

I suffered terribly for this lack of skill in taking heed to myself. I made others suffer, too. The most memorable experience of this was in my first appointment as a pastor. People had criticized my supposed lack of involvement with the youth of the church.

I did not objectively weigh their comments. I just set out to prove them wrong. I was entirely moved by what they said. I took no consideration for what I had done or needed to do. I simply involved myself with the youth that afternoon.

The problem was that I was supposed to be somewhere else. When I got back to the parsonage, there was a message on my machine. "Norm, where are you? We've got the largest crowd we've ever had. You are supposed to start the concert right now!" I felt sick—a common side effect of not taking heed of yourself. I had betrayed my commitment. I had been steered around by my bias to be right and prove others wrong. I couldn't blame anyone but myself.

This was not the only occasion this kind of thing happened to me. I warn you—develop the skill of taking heed to yourself. Otherwise, you will get worn out, burned out, and live on the edge of bitterness. There, you will not allow yourself to develop the next skill you need to live a life of breakthrough.

The King James Version shares the skills needed by those who are rooted to and revolve our living around accusation and blame. Take heed to yourselves and feed the flock.

Do not ever repeat the lie, "I have no ministry. I have no plan or purpose for my life." Do not repeat the lie, "I don't know what

I'm supposed to do with my life." Repeat with Jesus the universal truth, "I came not to be served, but to serve." Maybe you won't be called to give your life as a ransom for many. But you will need to develop the skill of feeding the flock among which the Holy Spirit has made you overseer.

What does it mean to feed your flock? It means you will learn how to love your neighbor as yourself. It means you are responsible for more than yourself. It means you will learn how to give a reason for the hope that is within you, communicating through word and deed the gospel of Jesus Christ.

Gary Chapman in his book, *The Five Love Languages,* shares five ways we can feed those whom the Holy Spirit has given us to oversee: words of affirmation, gifts, service, touch, and spending time together. The skill we're developing is to be innocent of only feeding others the way we like to be fed and being open to discovering the method or language of love that benefits best the other person.

We are taking heed to ourselves to make sure we do not love just to get loved in return. But we are actually developing the skill of feeding others because that will bless and strengthen them. This has to be done proactively. Otherwise, we will always be too busy.

I pray you never hear the words of indictment I heard from my son when he needed my help in fixing his bicycle. I told him I would help. He responded with the sad truth, "No, you won't, Daddy. You'll go to a meeting."

Be proactive. Develop the skill of taking heed to yourself but always in light of being able to have time and space to feed the flock over which God has made you an overseer. We develop this skill because we know something—life isn't fair. We love and feed those in our lives because we know others will take advantage of our neglect. We make the truth plain; most will distort it. We warn with tears because many will waylay those we love with temptation.

In this world, you shall have tribulation. Life is full of tragedy. There is plenty of fuel for fear and doubt. We understand that. Therefore, we become skilled in feeding faith. We become skilled in laying down our lives in the face of tragedy and disaster. Why? We know wolves can take on human form. We know that misery and mastery love company. We know people can easily become dependents rather than dependable. We know some desire to be masters more than ministers.

That is why we know we have to be commended to God and the word of his grace which is able to build us up. We know without this encouragement our relationships will break down with others. We will become reconciled to the distance and to the lack of expectations we develop over time. We will become discouraged and be tempted to point our fingers instead of proving our faith.

Determine right now the course you will follow. Will you point your finger in blame and give the wolves all the scapegoats they can devour? Or, will you arm yourself and open yourself to the responsibility-taking power of the Holy Spirit? Declare your innocence based on your love and faithfulness. Determine that you will be forthright and open in all your dealings. You will continue to grow and mature. You will not give in to escaping responsibility or looking for easy answers. The harder the situation, the more flexible you will be. You will be the first to forgive. You will move at the speed of grace!

MAP 4

God is speaking to you right now: "Aren't you excited? I've covered for all your expenses and accommodations. Every detail of the journey ahead is known by me. I will not leave you or forsake you. Don't be afraid. I'm going to be right beside you."

Yes, God is going to be right beside us as we map out this portion of the path. Remember the attitudes we are called to have describe the particular way we need to repent and believe. Answering this call will prove God is working everything together for our good. The skills we develop characterize the method we will use for building up our faith and blessing others. The knowledge under which we move forward encompasses the way God calls us to bring life and breakthrough for ourselves and for others. We can do it. We can move at the speed of grace.

> Now I commit you to God and to the word of his grace, which can build you up and give you an inheritance among all those who are sanctified. I have not coveted anyone's silver or gold or clothing. You yourselves know that these hands of mine have supplied my own needs and the needs of my companions. In everything I did, I showed you that by this kind of hard work we must help the weak, remembering the words the Lord Jesus himself said: "It is more blessed to give than to receive."
>
> Acts 20:32–35

The person called to follow this map has the most difficult path to walk. It is plain. It is a direct path, but it travels back to repentance through the other three. For this reason, rein yourself in under the command of Christ immediately. "Today, if you hear his voice, do not harden your hearts" (Hebrews 3:15). Resign yourself to follow Jesus as if you are the only one who will, all the while knowing everyone has to do the same. Take responsibility now for your choices. You are the only one who can. As Paul did, I commend you to God and to the word of his grace, but you will have to accept this commendation as your own before your life can change for the better.

That's why the attitude that begins a better life for you is an attitude of resignation to Jesus and the sufficiency of his grace. Up until now, you have resigned yourself to fears or the pain of abuse. You have papered the walls of your soul with the insults and limitations set for you by others. Their faithless comments have become the quotes you pasted on the mirror of your spirit. But, you have chosen a new interior decorator. His name is Jesus. There is no condemnation in him. He instead says, where I am there you may be also.

> Let us fix our eyes upon Jesus, the author and perfecter of our faith, who for the joy set before him endured the cross, scorning

its shame, and sat down at the right hand of God. Consider him who endured such opposition from sinful men, so that you will not grow weary and lose heart.

Hebrews 12:2–3

All of us have to choose each day what renews or refreshes our life. Imagine our life as a car on the road. What kind of air-freshener is hanging from our rearview mirror? Does it carry the stale, spoiled scent of yesterday's pain or are we riding along wrapped up in the far-reaching scent of God's joy and grace?

Can we count it all joy when hardships or trials have to be faced because we know this is the prism through which our faith is bent to display all of God's beauty?

To have this attitude of resignation, the Apostle Paul tells us there are some things we will have to let go: bitterness, rage and anger, brawling and slander, along with every form of malice. To maintain this attitude, we will have to be convinced kindness is more practical and better for our self interest than selfishness, compassion more practical than envy, forgiveness to be chosen over justifying ourselves, love more gratifying than lust, taking a wild step of faith safer than having no faith at all.

Yes, we need to be commended to God. Paul did it for the elders of the church at Ephesus. I commend you to God as you read this now. We all need a spiritual kick start. I need one. You need one. The real question is will we choose to make the present more important than the past? Will we allow the choices of today to be the key that redeems the choices made for us or that we made in the past?

We are committed to the word of God's grace. Our attitude is not only of resignation to Jesus and the sufficiency of his grace; our attitude is one of determination to walk the pathway of grace. God has made a way for us to be new creations where the old has passed away and behold (you can see it, too), everything is becoming new. We receive the gift of salvation.

A chief reason we are resigned and committed in our determination to God is we are in Jesus, not condemned to death or misery. God has not appointed us to wrath but to receive salvation through our Lord Jesus Christ. Even now, the blood of Jesus intercedes for us. Jesus lives and is committed to moving in our life, transforming us, healing us, restoring us by the power of his grace.

Yes, we are determined to walk in his ways and receive God's salvation. We are committed to forgiving the sins of those who hurt us or trespass against us. We owe no one anything but the love God has given us in Jesus Christ.

No one owes us anything—not even love—for our sufficiency is under the hand of God's grace. We are becoming what we were always meant to be: tender mercy incarnate, not resentment personified.

Now, when we are involved in something or with someone, things don't harden after we have passed through, but they are greener, softer, and more open to life than ever before. We move as one sent from above. The whisperings, "Speak of the devil," may still swirl around us, but they are no longer representative of who we are in Christ. We are determined and committed to walking in the light of God's word of grace. We focus and fasten on that.

We don't have a home on the plains where the deer and the antelope play. We often hear discouraging words, but we are no longer committed to fulfilling them. It may be cloudy all day, but we don't set our sights that low. We are guided by the word of his (you know who I'm talking about) grace that is able to build us up and give us a future that no one can take away.

Three years ago I paid money and entered into an authoring program that guaranteed I would finish authoring this book in six months or less. I was greatly helped by Glenn Dietzel at awakentheauthorwithin.com. Ronda DelBoccio, the Story Lady, was my coach. They provided me with great resources and encouragement. I didn't ask for my money back because it wasn't their fault I didn't finish in time. They gave me the tools that, if used, would have resulted in a finished book. But, I was too busy holding on to the sufficiency of my insufficiency.

Faithful determination was the attitude that enabled this book to happen. Without the attitude of determination, my pride or usual practice of starting and not finishing would not have waited for the grace to see the book through to its completion.

We are resigned and determined to follow Jesus and reflect his grace. We are thankful the word of grace builds us up. We understand that word of grace is needed because our biggest problem is not with God. It's with other people. We are tempted to echo the bumper sticker, "The more people I meet, the more I like my dog."

We keep our attitudes in place. Without them, we would quit before we start. With them in tact, Jesus is now leading us to develop skills that will make us functional and fruitful with God and others.

What are these skills? The first skill we develop as we follow Blueprint 4 is productive spiritual investing. We know developing the skill is not a wasted effort or expense. Jesus is leading us to a place of spiritual sufficiency and we have to learn some things to get there.

Spiritual investing meets the same objections as investing in the stock market. It's too risky. I don't have the resources to get started. It's too late to do me any good. We become resigned and committed to dullness and death instead of deliverance and development.

But, I know if you have come this far in the book, you have literally turned the page on following dead end commitments. You serve a Risen Savior. You have placed yourself at his feet. You are developing the skill of wise spiritual investments even if you have to unlearn everything to enjoy the inheritance God has determined to give you.

For that to happen, it has to be more than wishful thinking. There are action steps we can take to develop the skill of being wise investors. As Og Mandino, author of *The Greatest Salesman in the World,* says, "To become new I must form new habits and make myself their slave." To help us think about productive spiritual investing, I want to translate the first five investment principles (of seventeen) from Mark Tier's book, *The Winning Investment Habits of Warren Buffet and George Soros: Harness the Invest-*

ment Genius of the World's Richest Investors. I invite you to adopt and adapt these habits for yourself. Develop the skill of being a wise, spiritual investor.

1. "Preservation of capital is always priority #1." We preserve what we have received. We don't lose or waste what we have. We pay attention to our relationship with God. We do not neglect the gift of God. We are a citizen of God's kingdom. We don't give a beachhead to the enemy. We don't see how much we can get away with. We see how deep, wide, and far reaching our love and obedience can be. We know it is easier to maintain our reputation and our relationship with God than it is to get it back if it's lost or stolen.

2. "Passionately avoid risk." Concentrate on what you know. Don't give yourself to endless questions or speculations. Make choices, choose your friends, and set your schedule, so your faith and your future grow stronger. As Warren Buffett says: "Risk comes from not knowing what you are doing." "Study to show yourself approved, a workman that doesn't need to be ashamed, rightly dividing the word of truth" (2 Timothy 2:15).

3. "Develop your own unique investment philosophy." Decide how you will follow the pathway of grace. Which blueprint will be your guide? Who is your spiritual role model? How will you structure your praying? In what particular ways will you do justice, love mercy, and walk humbly with God? What or who, beyond yourself, will keep you in touch with reality?

4. "Develop your own personal system for selecting, buying, and selling investments." When a person begins investing in the stock market, he or she must keep it simple. The number one ingredient to that simplicity is for the person to understand what the product or service is in which he or

she is investing. In the same way, you discern and understand the voice of the Holy Spirit before you take action in ministry. Secondly, the product or service had to be exclusive or unique in how it met a particular need. Time, place, and price set guidelines on how I could invest. In the same way, you can't do everything in ministry but in given times and places, you can be the unique instrument of God. Where are those places for you? Do you know how to stand alert and ready for God to work through you? Thirdly, will there be a good return on my investment in this product or service? Is there a future benefit to taking action in the present? Spiritually, this is the place for the faith which works by love to engage itself. Evaluation can come later. Don't let feelings or uncertainty trump taking action. Proceed gently but proceed. You can always apologize and correct your mistake if mistakes are made. Love has got you covered.

5. "Buy as much as you can." Be unashamed of the good news of God's grace. Timidity and fear are enemies of ministry. When you have a conviction about actions you should take, take them! Exert your faith. Without faith, everything you do is sin, anyway (Romans 14:23). "Anyone, then, who knows the good he ought to do and doesn't do it, sins" (James 4:17). Work hard. Redeem the time. Become a wise, spiritual investor.

The skill that follows becoming a wise, spiritual investor is the skill of becoming a wise, spiritual philanthropist. We are developing the skill of giving. How do we measure our success? We determine where we can best give to bring out the best in others.

Paul says we work hard so that we can help the weak. We build ourselves up, so we can bless others. We give and live from the depth and wealth of our investments. I'm glad I didn't finish this book three years ago. What I could give to you would be far less or call for a second book if I had finished then.

You made an investment and bought this book. I'm praying you will develop a greater ministry and provide a better gift and return to others by reading it than I can. You have friends that I don't have. The smallest lesson coming from you will be greater than anything I can teach them.

You can develop your skill for giving. Work your soul like the good soil it is. Prepare yourself for giving. Tithe. Budget your income. Commend yourself to God and to the word of his grace.

Plan and plant your giving into the kingdom of God and into the lives of others. Plan it so that your generous self and not your stingy self determines what your giving is. Plan it so that the Holy Spirit can speak faith into your obedience and fear can't turn you into a tight wad.

Review your giving from time to time. What is the most effective use of your resources? How can Jesus be exalted in your giving? Prune your spending and giving decisions. You are not called to do everything but to be wholehearted in everything you do. Look for secret ways you can bless others. Give without expecting anything in return.

Paul says we develop the skills of investing and giving because we know we are to help the weak. This is one of the guiding principles of our faith. In Galatians 2:10 Paul said that remembering the poor or helping the weak was the one overarching characteristic that accompanied the proclamation of the gospel. The first Church Council apparently affirmed remembering the poor or helping the weak as the one positive command it placed upon Jew and Gentile convert alike.

Finally, Paul says we develop the skills of investing and giving, maintain our attitudes of resignation and determination because we have the words of Jesus. We know it is more blessed to give than to receive.

One reason that is true is because giving means we have already received. God's grace is sufficient for us. We know the blessing and counsel of God. We know how God has changed our life. We know God has saved us. Certainly, we want others to know these things, too.

There is a song that I learned as a little boy at Vacation Bible School. These are the words:

> Christ's is my way through weather fair or stormy.
> Onward He leads me, his banner goes before me.
> Others have served him and found him to be true.
> Yes, Christ's is my way. It should be your way, too.

Let this be your song. Let this be your prayer. "Teach me your way, O Lord, and I will walk in your truth; give me an undivided heart that I may fear your name" (Psalm 86:11).

Scripture Reading from 1 King 13

The attitude of reliance must always be yoked to the attitude of obedience. You cannot walk the pathway of grace unless they are joined together. This is graphically illustrated here in 1 Kings 13. Read this chapter and see the life and death reasons why the attitudes of reliance and obedience are yoked together as you follow Map 2.

THE MAN OF GOD FROM JUDAH

By the word of the LORD a man of God came from Judah to Bethel, as Jeroboam was standing by the altar to make an offering. He cried out against the altar by the word of the LORD: "O altar, altar! This is what the LORD says: 'A son named Josiah will be born to the house of David. On you he will sacrifice the priests of the high places who now make offerings here, and human bones will be burned on you.'" That same day the man of God gave a sign: "This is the sign the LORD has declared: The altar will be split apart and the ashes on it will be poured out."

When King Jeroboam heard what the man of God cried out against the altar at Bethel, he stretched out his hand from the altar and said, "Seize him!" But the hand he stretched out toward the man shriveled up, so that he could not pull it back. Also, the altar was split apart, and its ashes poured out according to the sign given by the man of God by the word of the LORD.

Then the king said to the man of God, "Intercede with the LORD your God and pray for me that my hand may be restored." So the man of God interceded with the LORD, and the king's hand was restored and became as it was before.

The king said to the man of God, "Come home with me and have something to eat, and I will give you a gift."

But the man of God answered the king, "Even if you were to give me half your possessions, I would not go with you, nor would I eat bread or drink water here. For I was commanded by the word of the LORD: 'You must not eat bread or drink water or return by the way you came.'" So he took another road and did not return by the way he had come to Bethel.

Now there was a certain old prophet living in Bethel, whose sons came and told him all that the man of God had done there that day. They also told their father what he had said to the king. Their father asked them, "Which way did he go?" And his sons showed him which road the man of God from Judah had taken. So he said to his sons, "Saddle the donkey for me." And when they had saddled the donkey for him, he mounted it and rode after the man of God. He found him sitting under an oak tree and asked, "Are you the man of God who came from Judah?"

"I am," he replied.

So the prophet said to him, "Come home with me and eat."

The man of God said, "I cannot turn back and go with you, nor can I eat bread or drink water with you in this place. I have been told by the word of the LORD: 'You must not eat bread or drink water there or return by the way you came.'"

The old prophet answered, "I too am a prophet, as you are. And an angel said to me by the word of the LORD: 'Bring him back with you to your house so that he may eat bread and drink water.'" (But he was lying to him.) So the man of God returned with him and ate and drank in his house.

While they were sitting at the table, the word of the LORD came to the old prophet who had brought him back. He cried out to the man of God who had come from Judah, "This is what the LORD says: 'You have defied the word of the LORD and have not kept the command the LORD your God gave you. You came back and ate bread and drank water in the place where he told you not to eat or drink. Therefore your body will not be buried in the tomb of your fathers.'"

When the man of God had finished eating and drinking, the prophet who had brought him back saddled his donkey for him. As he went on his way, a lion met him on the road and killed him, and his body was thrown down on the road, with both the donkey and the lion standing beside it. Some people who passed by saw the body thrown down there, with the lion standing beside the body, and they went and reported it in the city where the old prophet lived.

When the prophet who had brought him back from his journey heard of it, he said, "It is the man of God who defied the word of the LORD. The LORD has given him over to the lion, which has mauled him and killed him, as the word of the LORD had warned him."

The prophet said to his sons, "Saddle the donkey for me," and they did so. Then he went out and found the body thrown down on the road, with the donkey and the lion standing beside it. The lion had neither eaten the body nor mauled the donkey. So the prophet picked up the body of the man of God, laid it on the donkey, and brought it back to his own city to mourn for him and bury him. Then he laid the body in his own tomb, and they mourned over him and said, "Oh, my brother!"

After burying him, he said to his sons, "When I die, bury me in the grave where the man of God is buried; lay my bones beside his bones. For the message he declared by the word of the LORD against the altar in Bethel and against all the shrines on the high places in the towns of Samaria will certainly come true."

Even after this, Jeroboam did not change his evil ways, but

once more appointed priests for the high places from all sorts of people. Anyone who wanted to become a priest he consecrated for the high places. This was the sin of the house of Jeroboam that led to its downfall and to its destruction from the face of the earth.

BIBLIOGRAPHY

Bonhoeffer, Dietrich. *The Cost of Discipleship.* New York: MacMillan Publishing Company, 1963.

Bowen, C. A., editor. *The Cokesbury Worship Hymnal.* Baltimore, The Methodist Publishing House, 1938.

Chapman, Gary. *The Five Love Languages.* Chicago: Northfield Publishing, 2004.

Cordeiro, Wayne. *Life Journal.* Hong Kong: New Hope International, 2003.

Eldredge, John. *The Way of the Wild Heart (Fathered by God).* Nashville: Thomas Nelson, Inc., 2006.

Fisher, Ken. *The Only Three Questions That Count.* Hoboken, NJ: John Wiley & Sons, Inc., 2007.

Institute of Arbinger. *Leadership and Self-Deception.* San Francisco: Berrett-Koehler Publishers, 2002.

Mandino, Og. *The Greatest Salesman in the World.* New York: Bantam, 1983.

Ramsey, Dave. *Financial Peace.* New York: Viking Penguin., 1997

Ramsey, Dave. *Total Money Makeover.* Nashville: Thomas Nelson, Inc., 2003

Tier, Mark. *The Winning Investment Habits of Warren Buffett and George Soros.* New York: St. Martin's Press, 2006.